I0390739

flaminio gundy

Cortina

The pearl of Dolomites

Cortina
The pearl of Dolomites

by Flaminio Gundy

All rights reserved.
No part of this book may be used or reproduced in any manner without written permission of the publisher.

Copyright © 2019 by Flaminio Gundy

Kindle Direct Publishing, USA, 2019

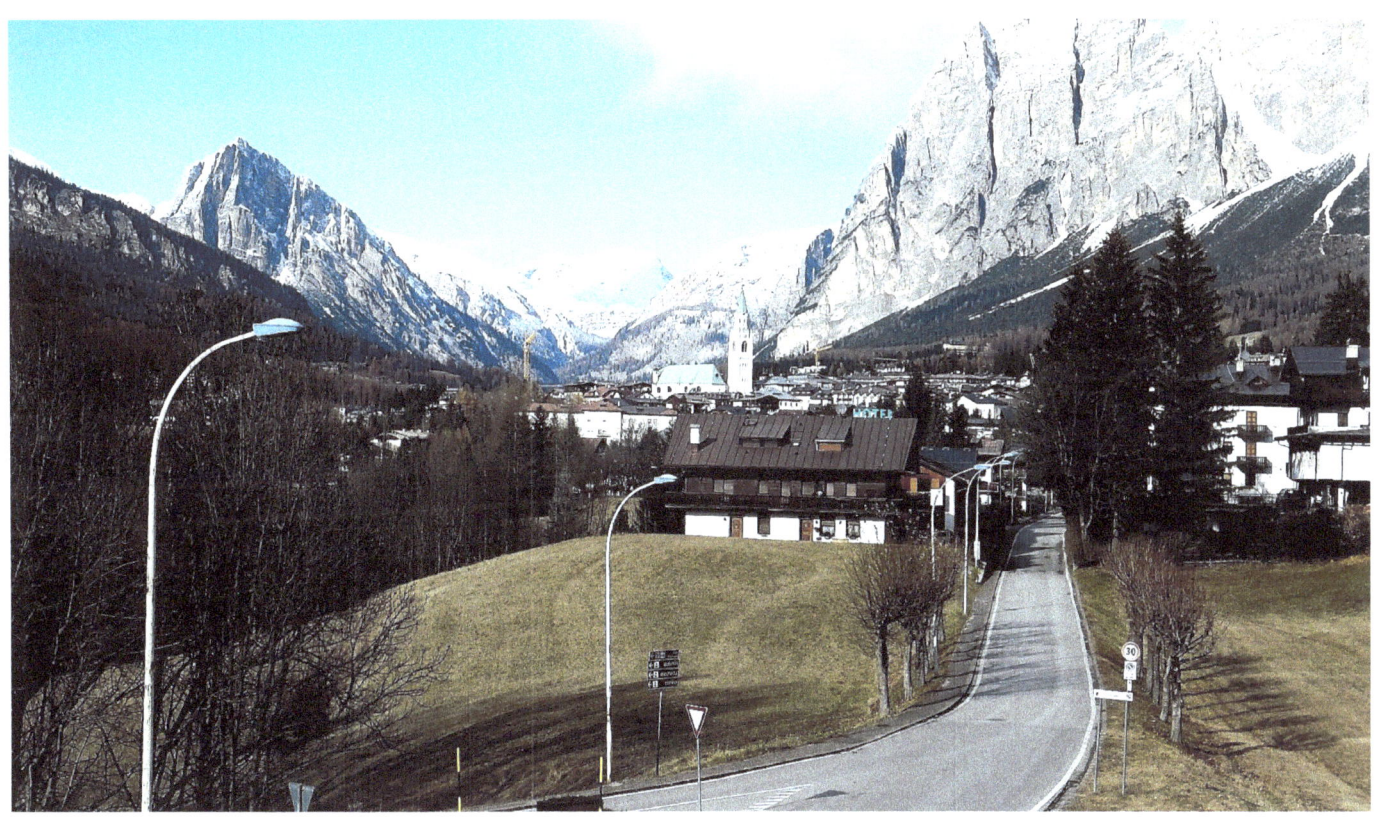

Cortina rises in the center of the Conca Ampezzana, in the upper valley of the Boite stream, and belongs to the province of Belluno (Veneto Region). It is entirely surrounded by the Ampezzo Dolomites, which include the Tofane and Cristallo group, Punta Sorapiss, Becco di Mezzodì, Croda da Lago and the Nuvolau group.

Under the rule of the Habsburgs for five centuries, from 1511 to 1918, **Cortina** became a favorite holiday resort of the middle European nobility in the second half of the 19th century, experiencing a sort of golden age when the neighboring Cadore suffered poverty and emigration. After fighting the Great War with the Austro-Hungarian uniform, the Cortinesi hesitantly accepted the arrival of General Cadorna's troops in 1915 and the annexation to the Kingdom of Italy at the end of hostility.

The majority of the population of **Cortina** speak the ampezzano, a local variant of Ladin, a Romance language derived from Latin (such as Italian, French, Romanian, Sardinian, Spanish and Portuguese).

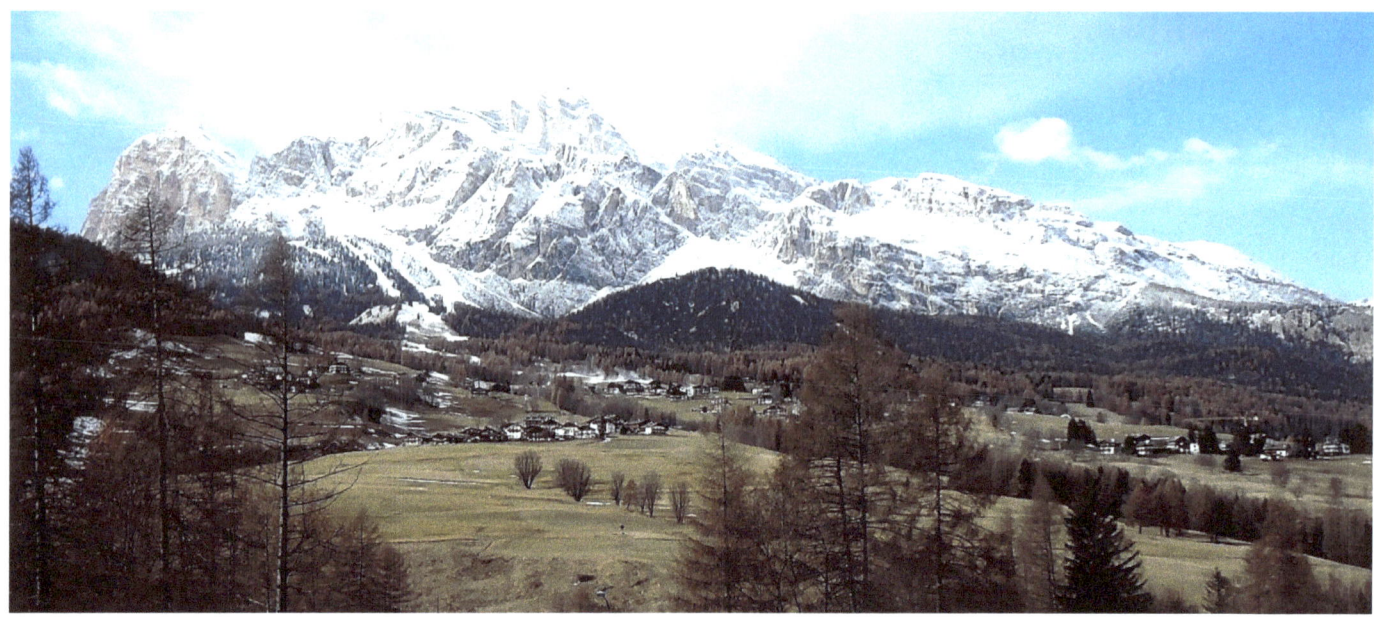
Tofane

For historical reasons the Ampezzo cuisine reflects strong ties with the Tyrolean gastronomy and it is always food from the popular tradition, generally poor, but rich in flavor and tradition.

Bigoli con anatra, first course of fresh handmade pasta, in particular spaghetti rather thick bronze drawn. They are made with eggs, flour, butter, water and salt. They should not be cooked in boiling water but in duck fat broth and then seasoned with herb butter and duck giblets.

Casunzièi, crescent-shaped ravioli stuffed with beetroot and potato. They go hand-prepared and served with a sauce made with butter and smoked ricotta, the so-called *spersada*. It is a simple but very tasty dish, a real delicacy. Peel and grate the potatoes, cook them in a pan with a knob of butter for about 15 minutes, then leave to cool and place in a bowl.
Add the ricotta, mascarpone, salt, pepper and grated nutmeg and mix well until dough is smooth. Roll out the sheets of pasta and cut of about 8 cm to 12 cm rectangles. Place the center of everyone a spoon of stuffing and fold it lengthwise, pressing the edges with moistened fingers to not let out the stuffing. Slightly bend the ends of *casunziei* to give them their characteristic arched shape. Cook them in salted water for five minutes, drain and toss with the melted butter. Finally sprinkle with fresh ricotta cheese into cubes and serve.

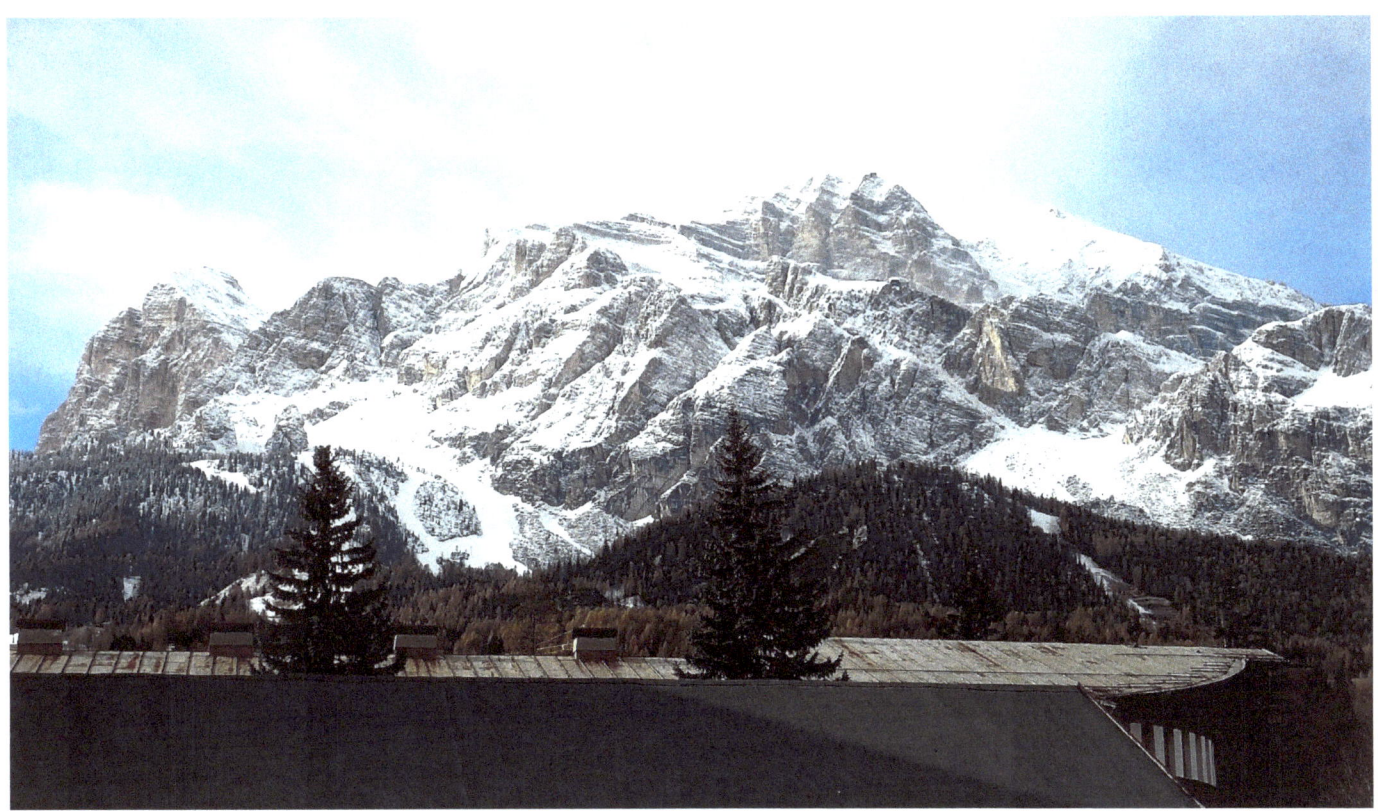

Tofane

Chenédi, Ampezzana dumplings. Beat the eggs with the milk and a pinch of pepper in a bowl, add the diced stale bread and let stand for a few minutes, stirring occasionally. Add the speck cut into strips and then coarsely chopped, the diced salami, the chopped chives, the finely chopped parsley, a pinch of salt and grated nutmeg. Stir in the flour a little at a time, stirring carefully until the mixture is not too moist. With wet hands, make little balls as big as walnuts and pass them in the boiling broth for a dozen minutes. Meanwhile, dice the lard and the remaining speck into strips, browning them separately first one and then the other in a non-stick pan. Drain the *chenédi*, drip them a few moments and arrange them on a hot plate. At this point you can dress them with lard, speck and chives to taste.

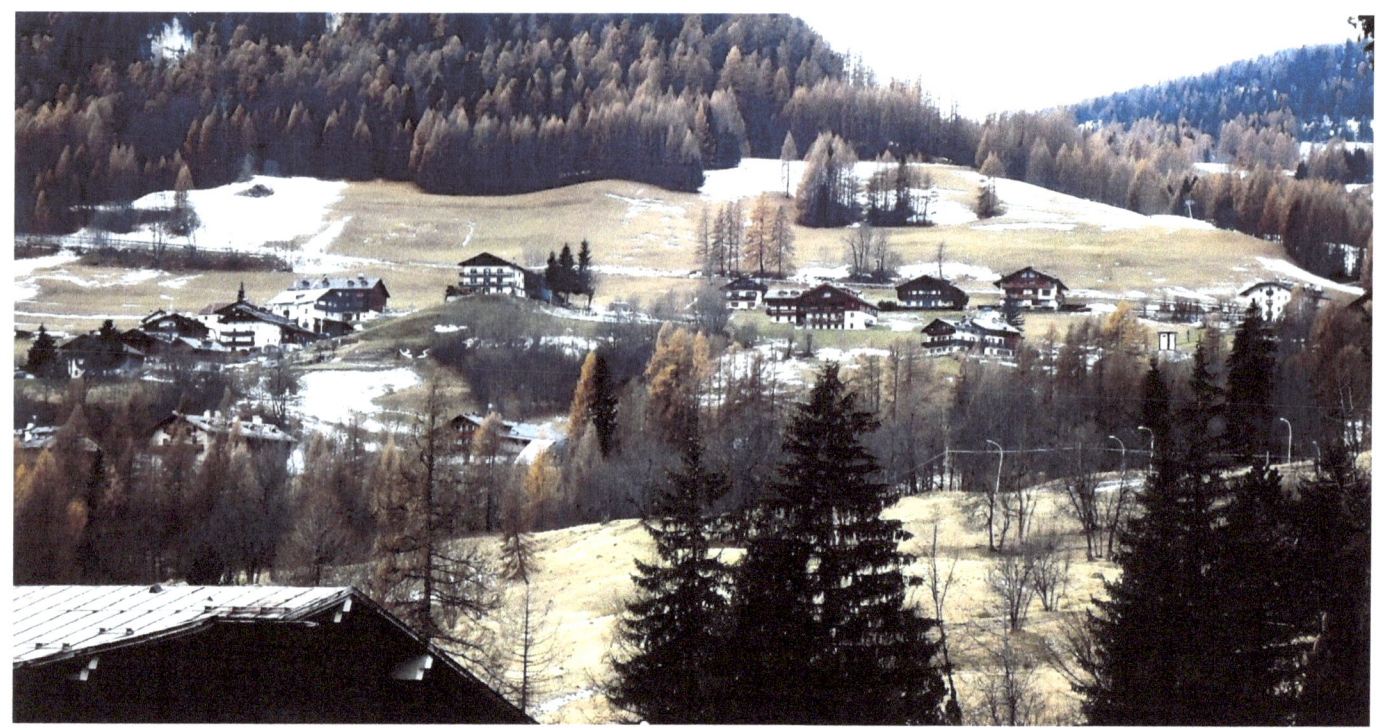

Gnocchi di ricotta fresca, mix the ricotta with the whole eggs, egg yolks, flour, salt and some parmesan. Form the gnocchi with spoon, boil them in salted water for a few minutes and season directly in the bowl with little parmesan and brown butter.

Minestra di patate e funghi, wash the potatoes, cover them in a pot with water and boil for about 30 minutes. Drain and let them cool and peel them. Crumble with your hands and place them in a saucepan, add the milk, two glasses of water and a pinch of salt thoroughly stirring with a wooden spoon. Scrape the mushrooms to remove any earth residues, wipe them with a damp cloth without washing them and cut them into thin slices with a boxcutter. In a saucepan melt the butter, add the mushrooms and chopped onion. Left to wither for about 15 minutes until they are soft and season with salt. Boil the potatoes with the milk, add the onions and stewed mushrooms, stirring well to mix. Cook for 10 minutes. Finely chop the parsley, thyme, marjoram and add them to the soup after cooking.

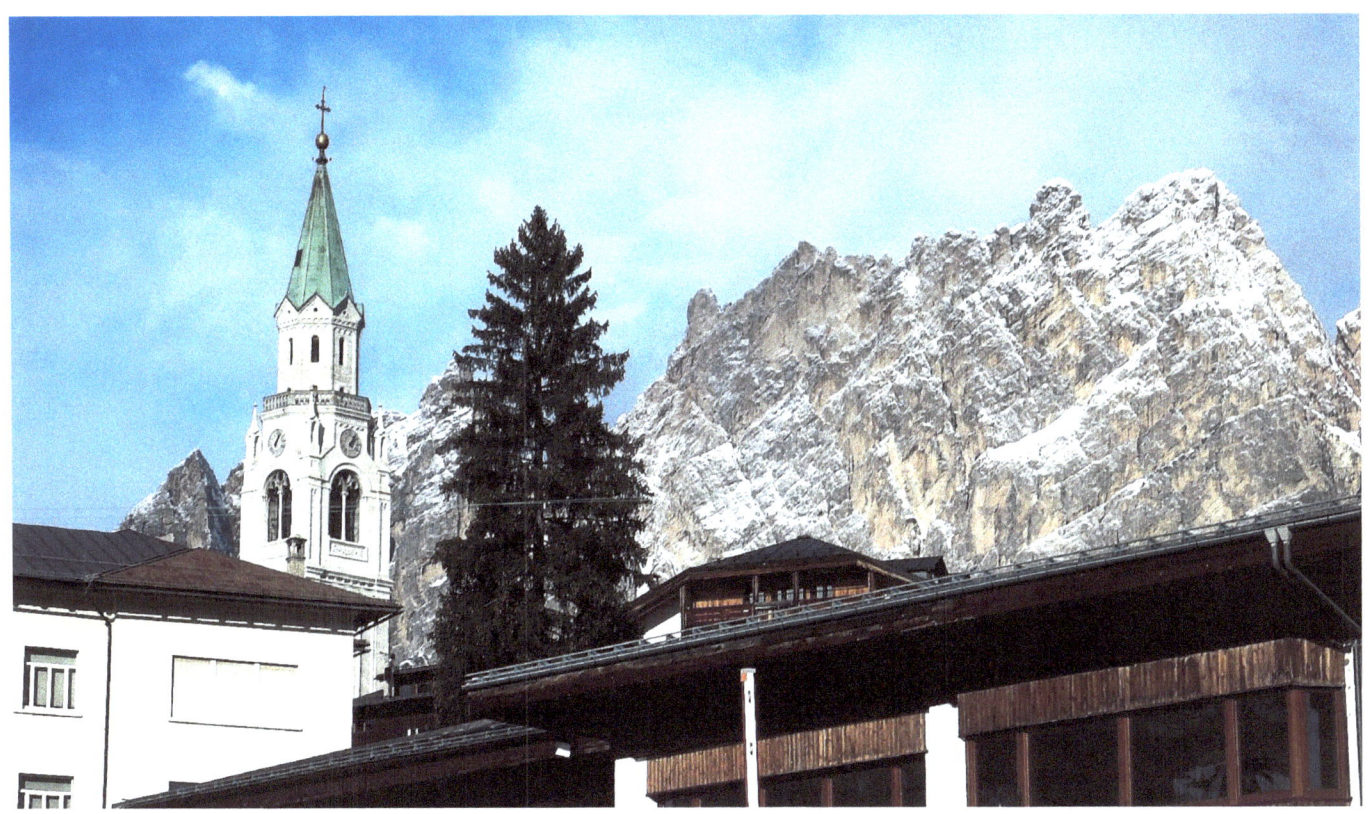

Paparelle con piselli, dice the bacon and chopped onions. Put everything in a pan with a knob of butter, then add the peas, broth and salt to taste. Cook on low heat with covered vessel for about 20 minutes: at the end the peas will be tender and the broth must be almost completely absorbed. Chop the parsley and set aside. Cook the *paparelle* in salted water and drain when al dente. Add other butter to the peas, stir and sprinkle with parsley and grated parmesan cheese.

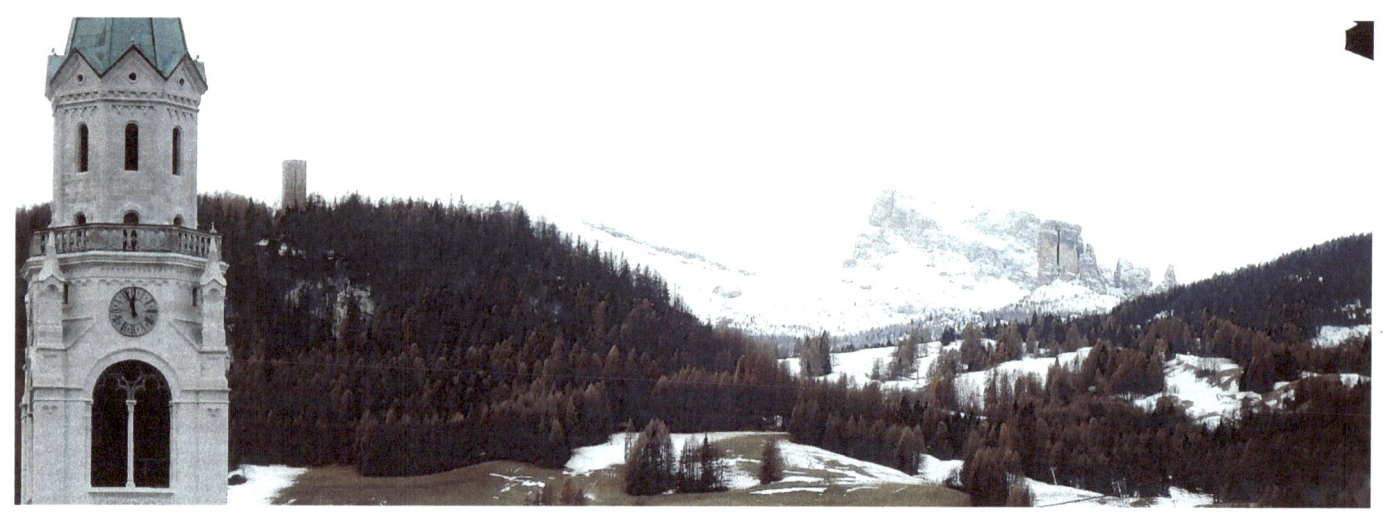

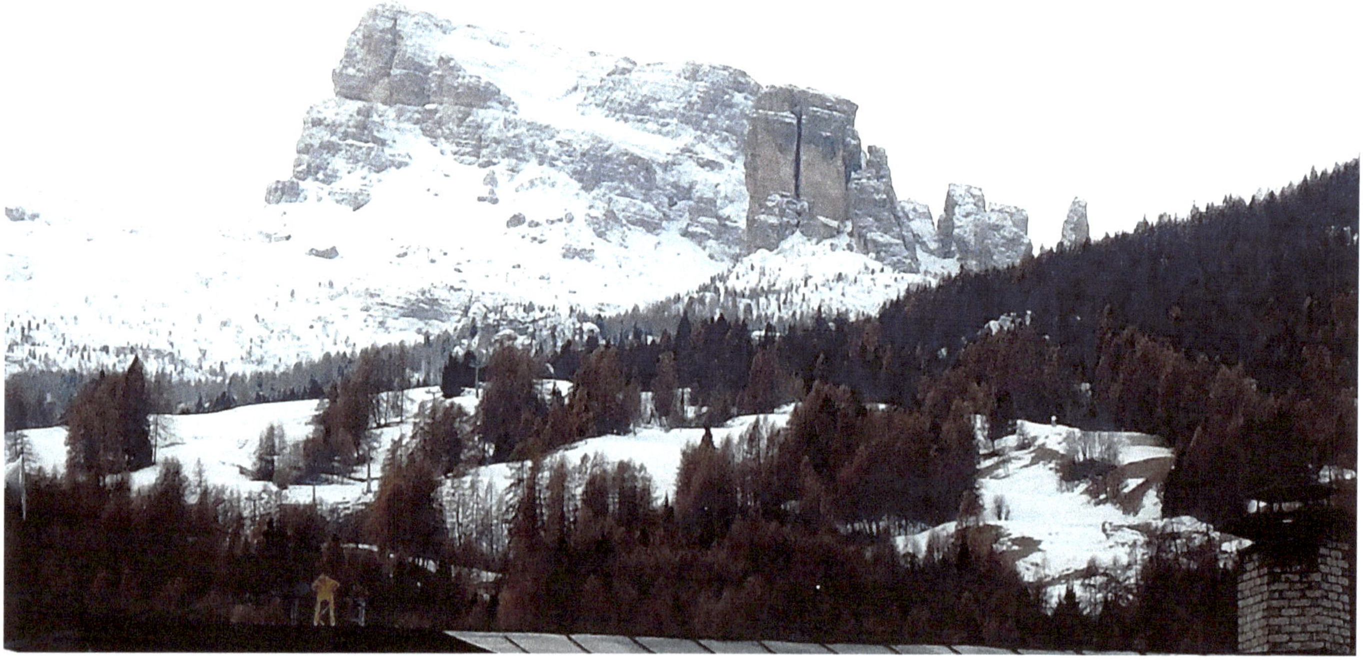

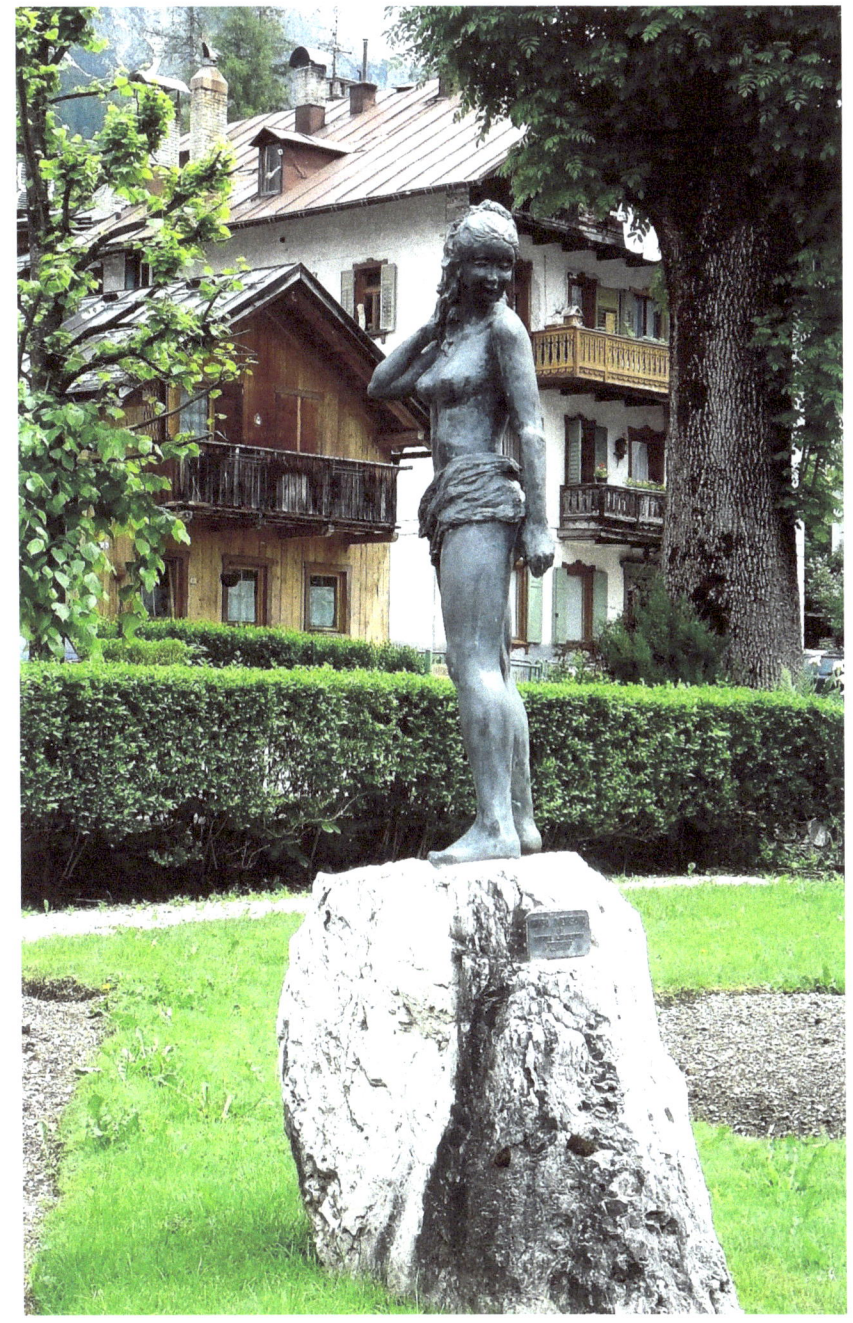

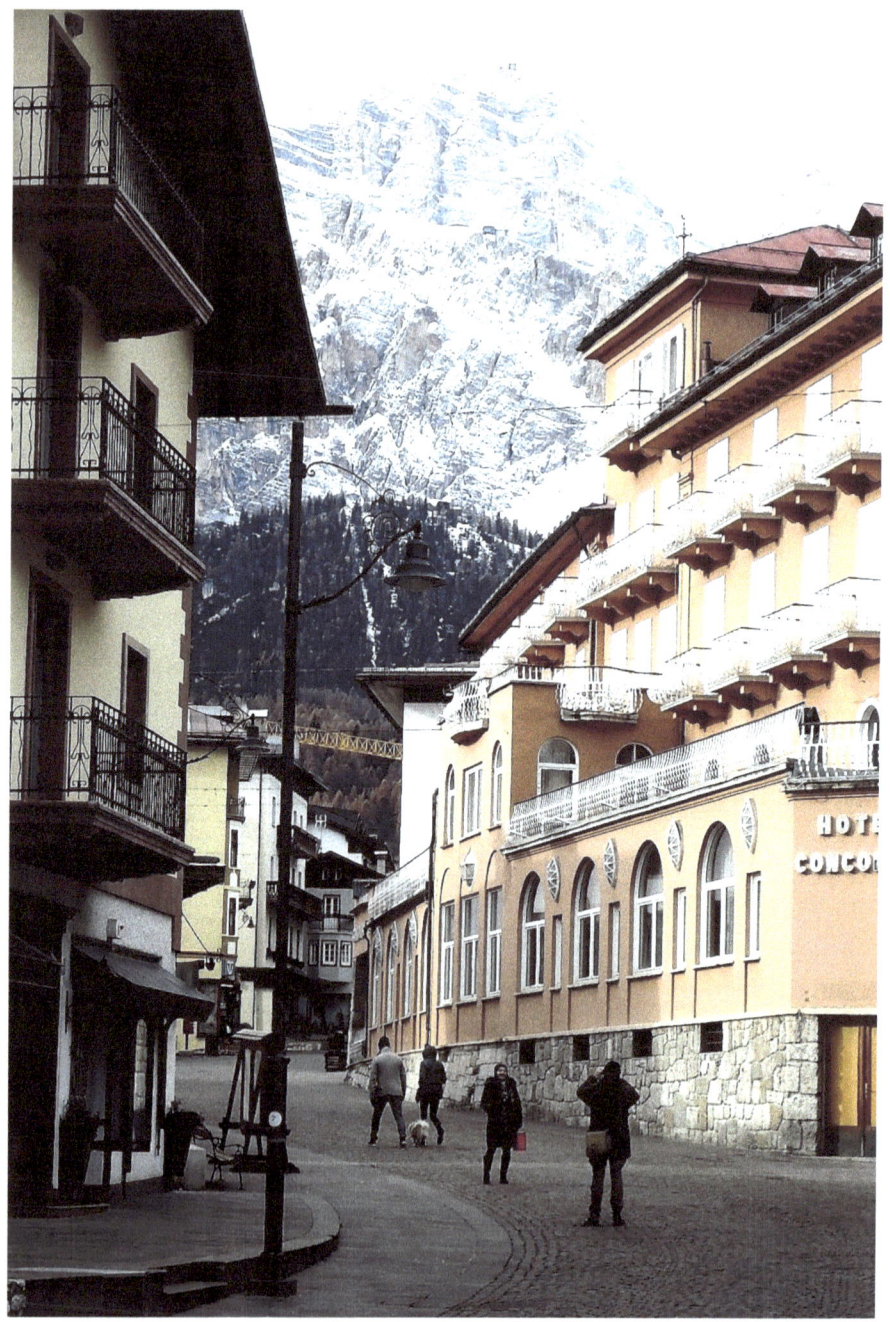

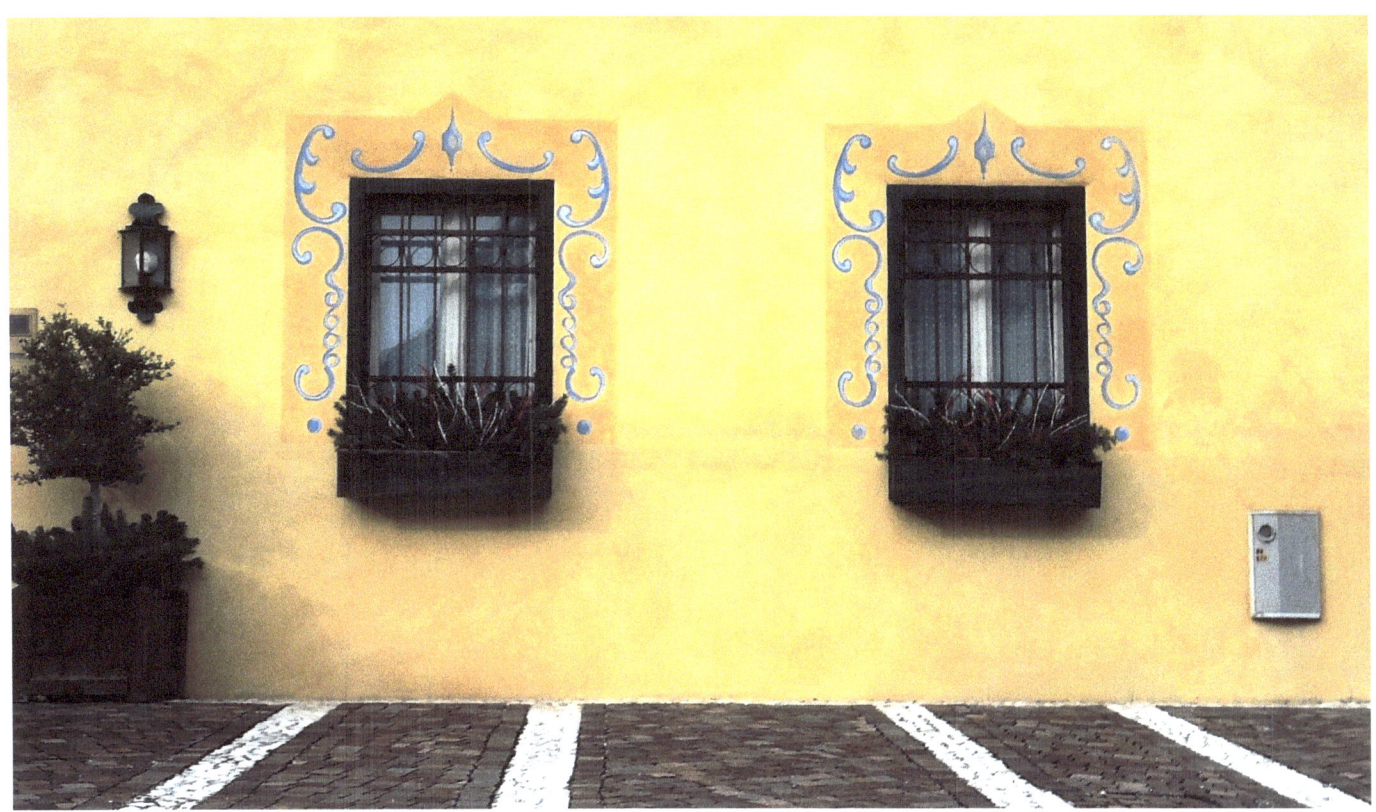

Pendolón, rich soup made with beans and potatoes. Boil the potatoes, peel them and let them cool. Boil Lamon beans or borlotti and finely chopped onions. Put the lard or fresh butter in a copper pot and brown the chopped onion. After a few minutes, add the cooked potatoes and mash them with force, using a wooden spoon until a smooth paste. Add the cooked beans, without crush them all, add salt and pepper to taste. Stir for a few minutes over low heat, adding a few knobs of butter. At the end pour the dough on a cutting board and let cool, obtaining at this point the slices like a normal polenta. The ***pendolón*** is eaten either hot or cold, cut in thick slices as a finger.

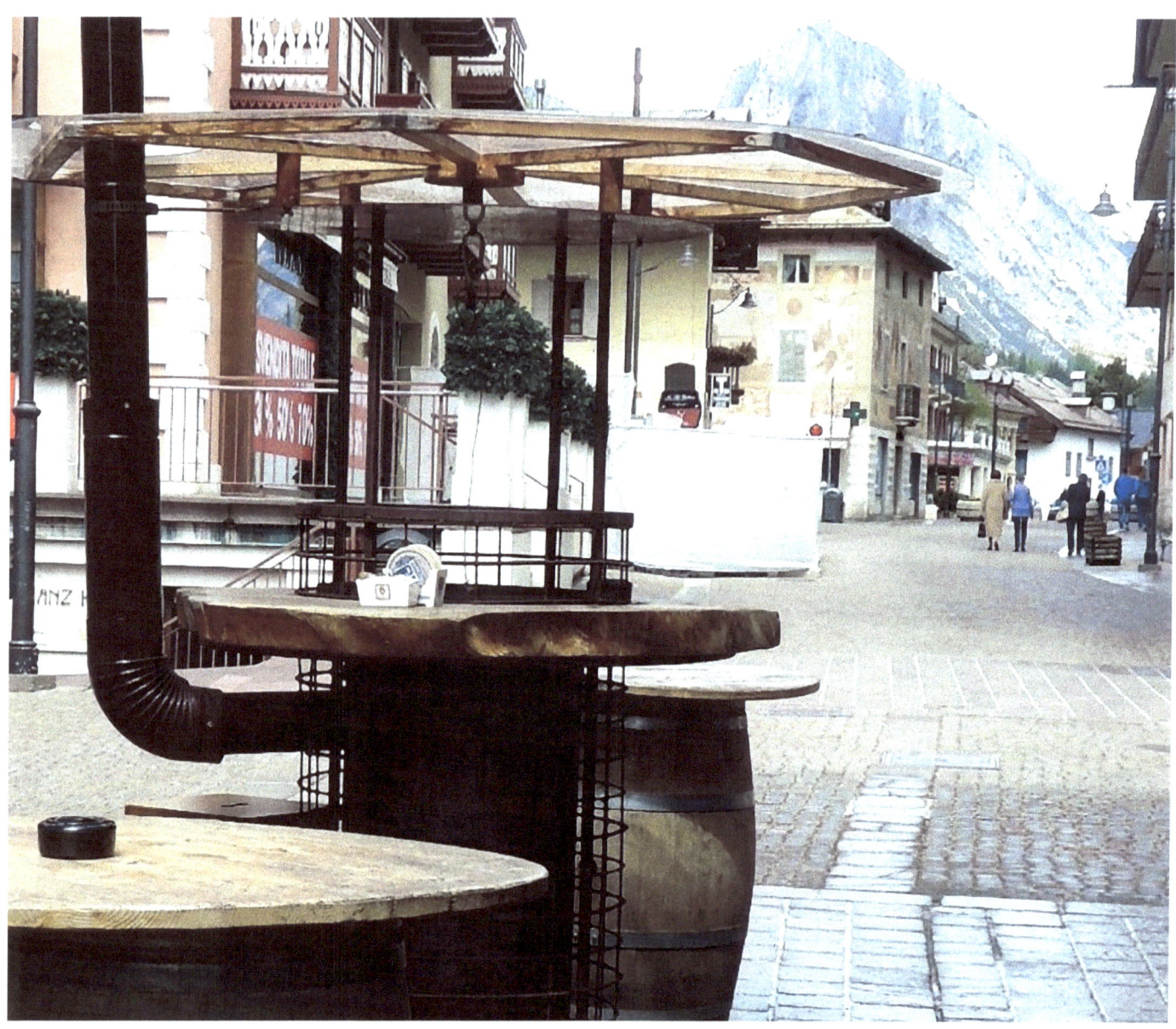

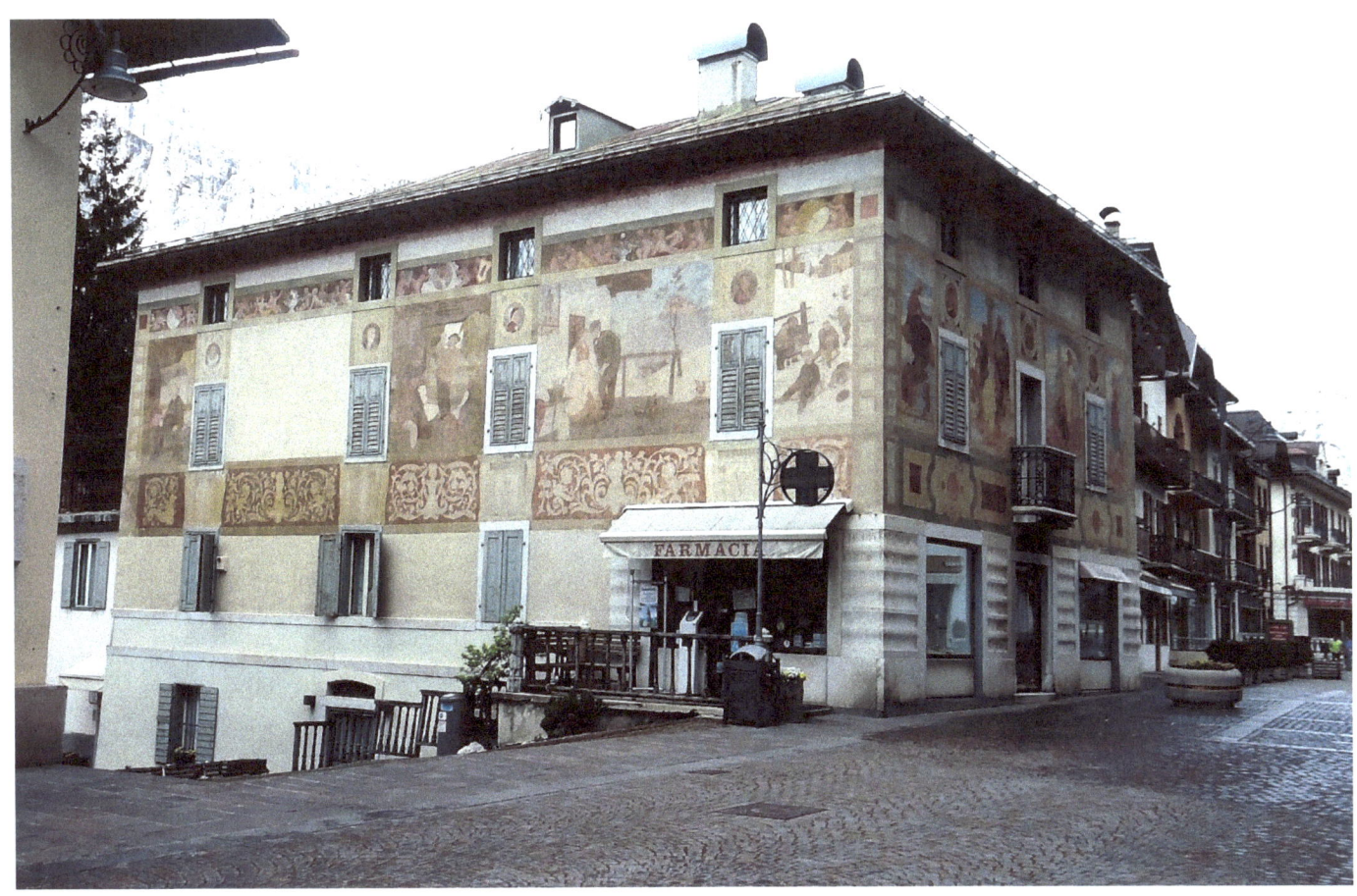

Polenta pastissada, pour 2 liters of water in a copper pot, add salt and put on the fire. As the water begins to boil, slowly add the flour, stirring constantly with a wooden spoon. Continue cooking for about 40 minutes while continuing to stir to avoid lumps. At the end of cooking carefully roll out the polenta on a damp floor or marble and flatten to obtain the thickness of about one centimeter. Once cooled cut it into slices...

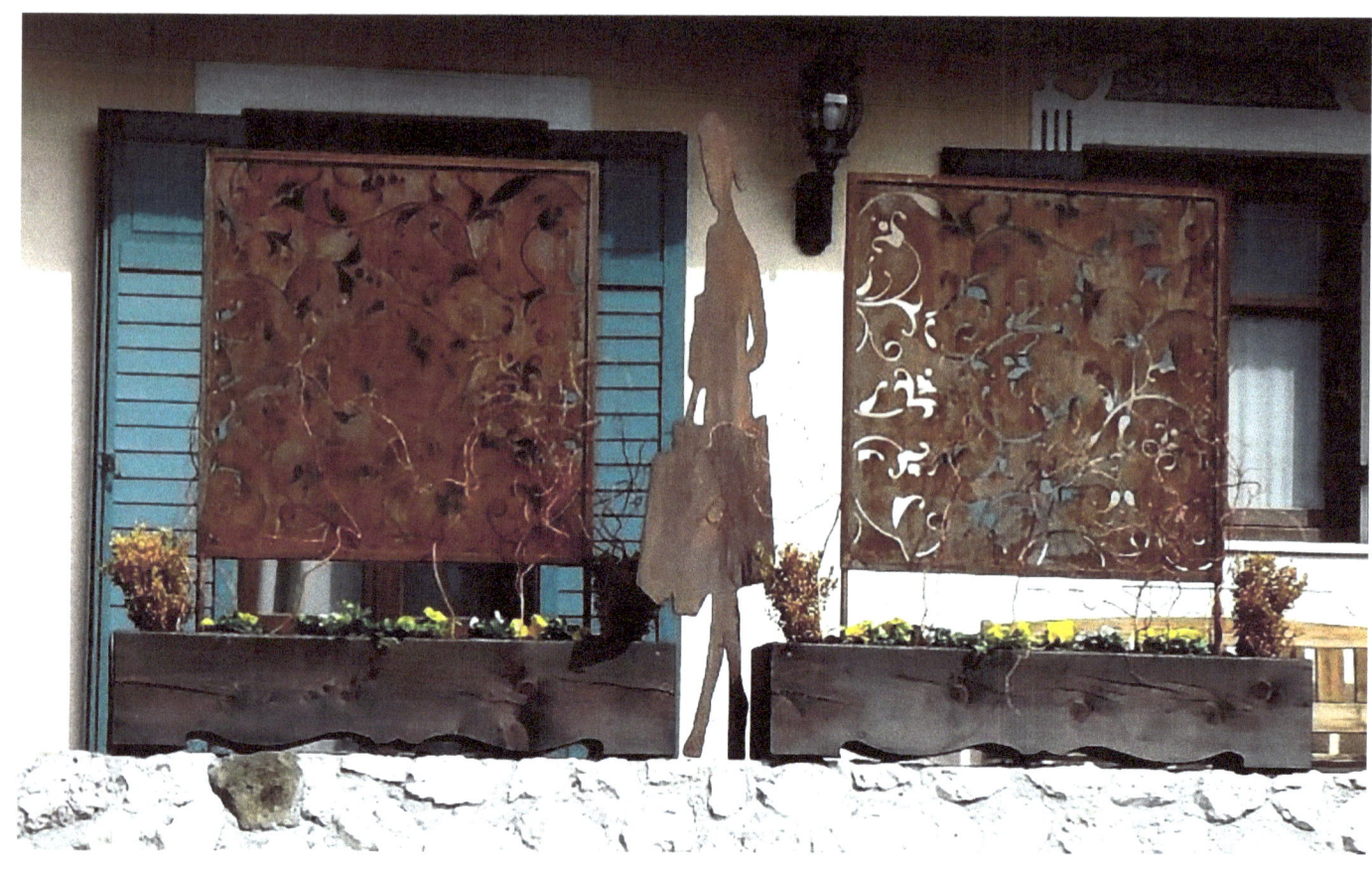

...Wash the chicken giblets and fry in a pan with the butter, then chop them. Chop together the onion with garlic, carrot and celery, pour into a saucepan and fry with a little oil. Dice the ham not too small, then add it to browned with the giblets and ground beef and sear it all. Pour the white wine to the pan and let it evaporate over low heat. Add the tomato puree, salt and pepper and continue cooking for about 30 minutes. Anoint with oil a baking dish, arrange a layer of polenta and sprinkle with sauce and cheese. Repeat the layers, crossing every time the arrangement of slices compared to the previous layer and finish with cheese. Bake in oven 200° C for about 20 minutes until on the surface will have formed a nice golden crust.

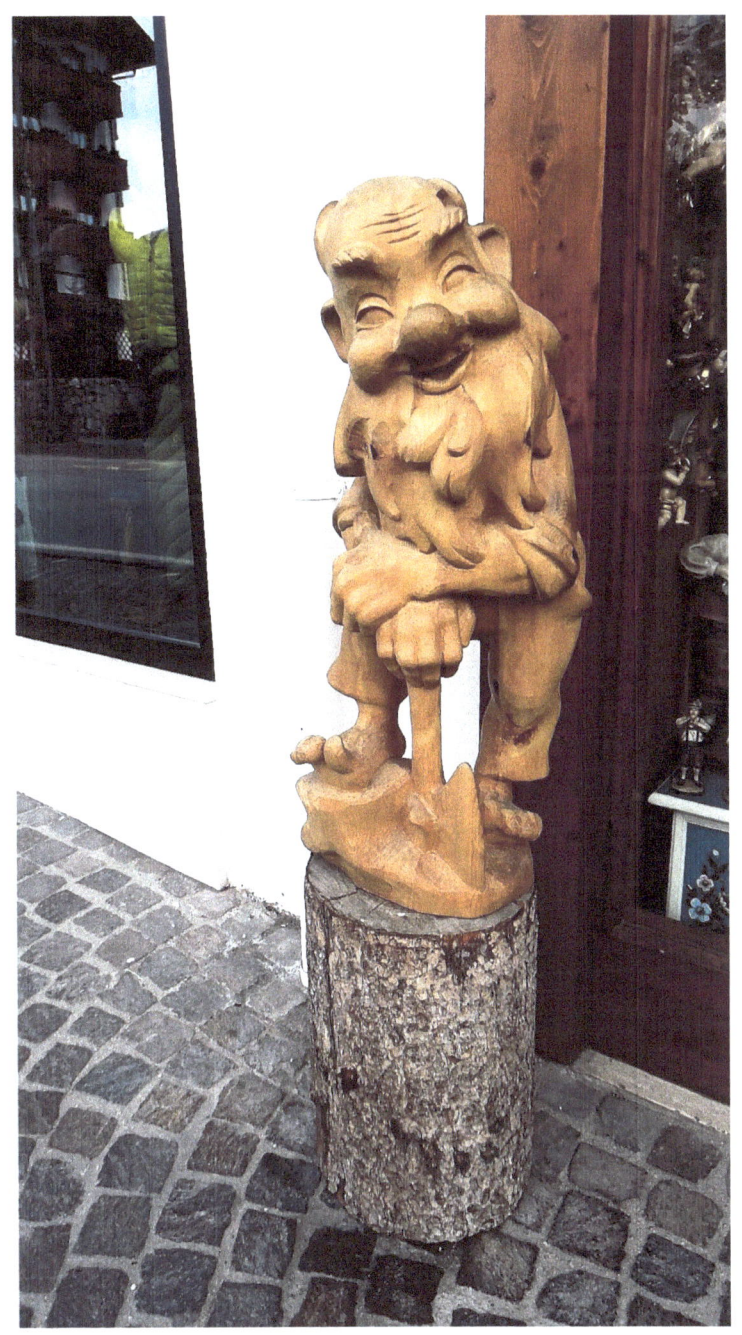

15

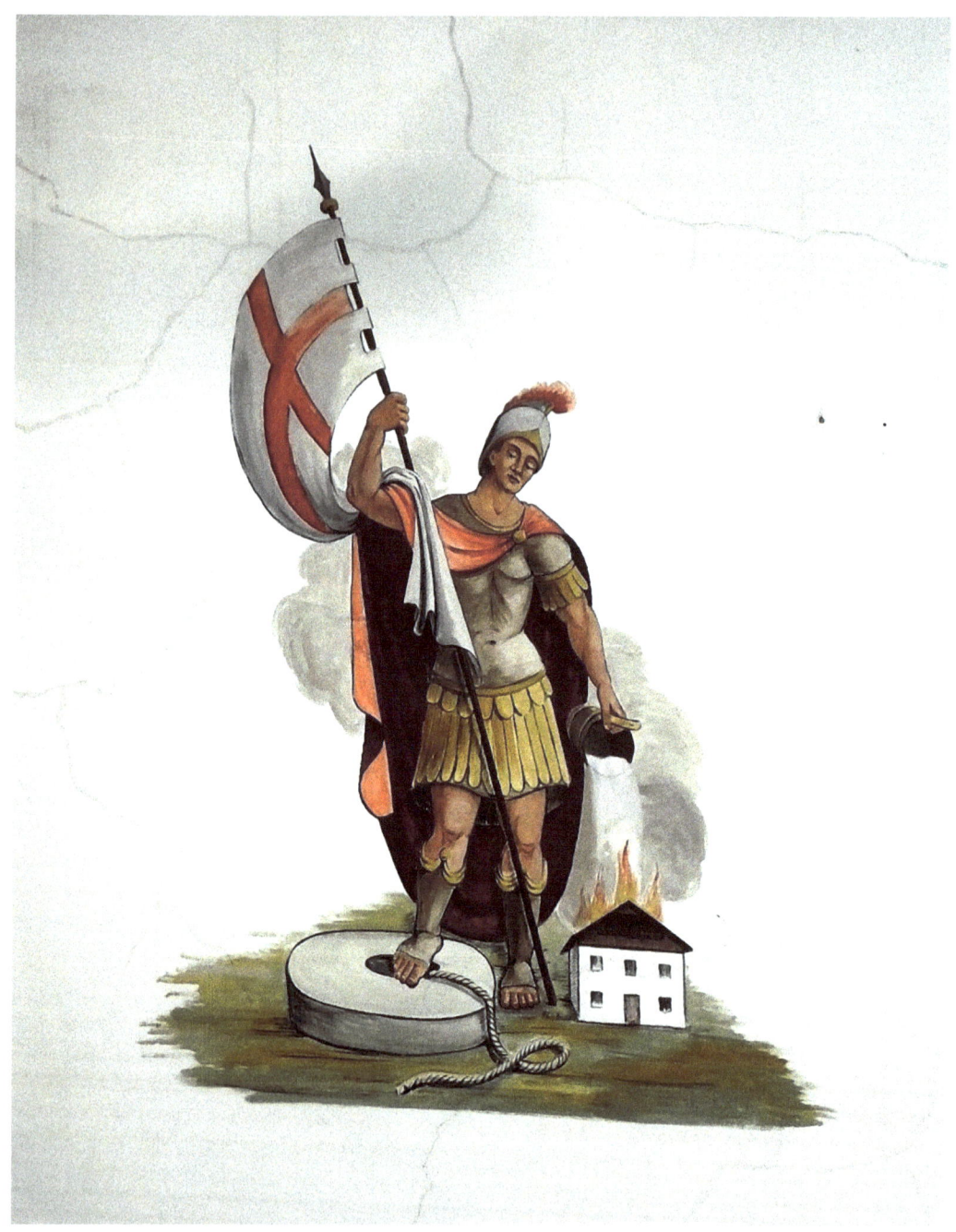

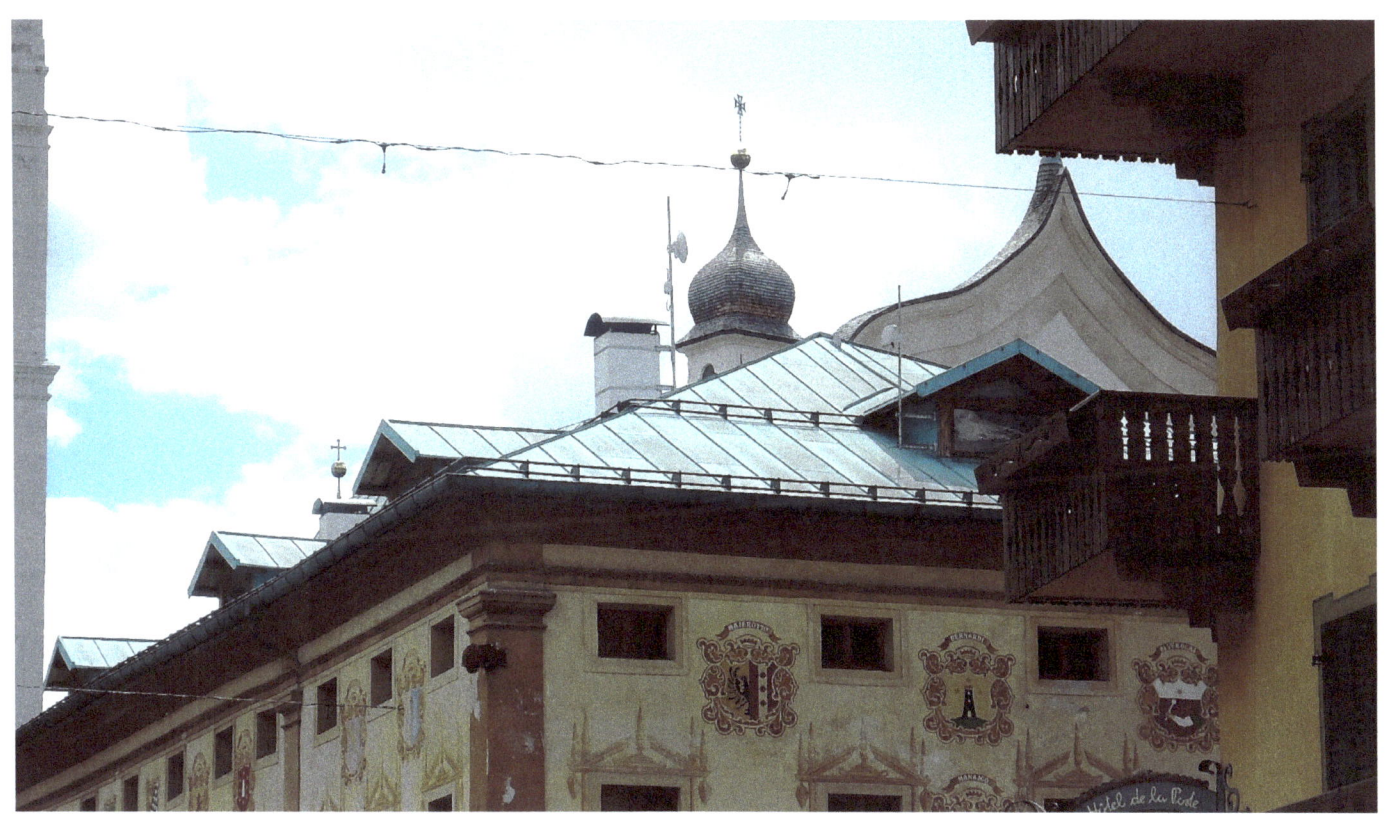

Risotto con funghi, make wither in olive oil a chopped leek side, add a clove of garlic and a bay leaf. Pour the mushrooms, let them cook and when they are cooked add the rice, moisten it with half a glass of dry white wine, let it evaporate and add a little at a time the broth. A few minutes before the end of cooking knead adding fresh butter, Parmesan cheese and chopped parsley.

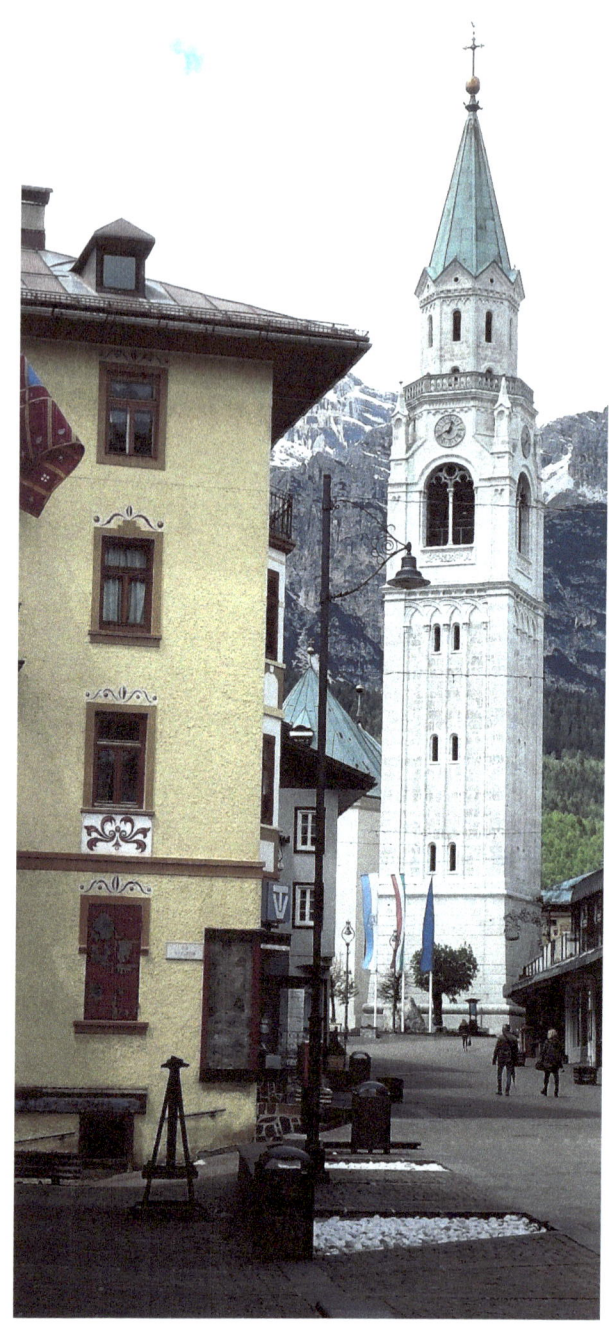

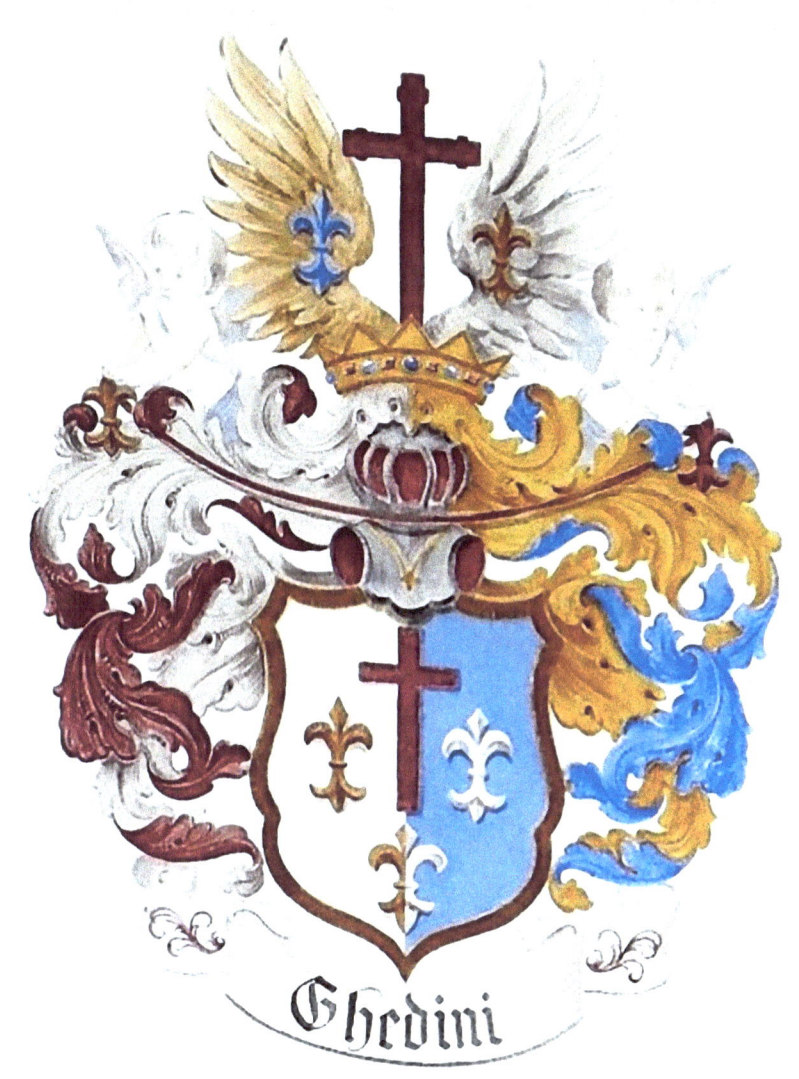

Ghedini

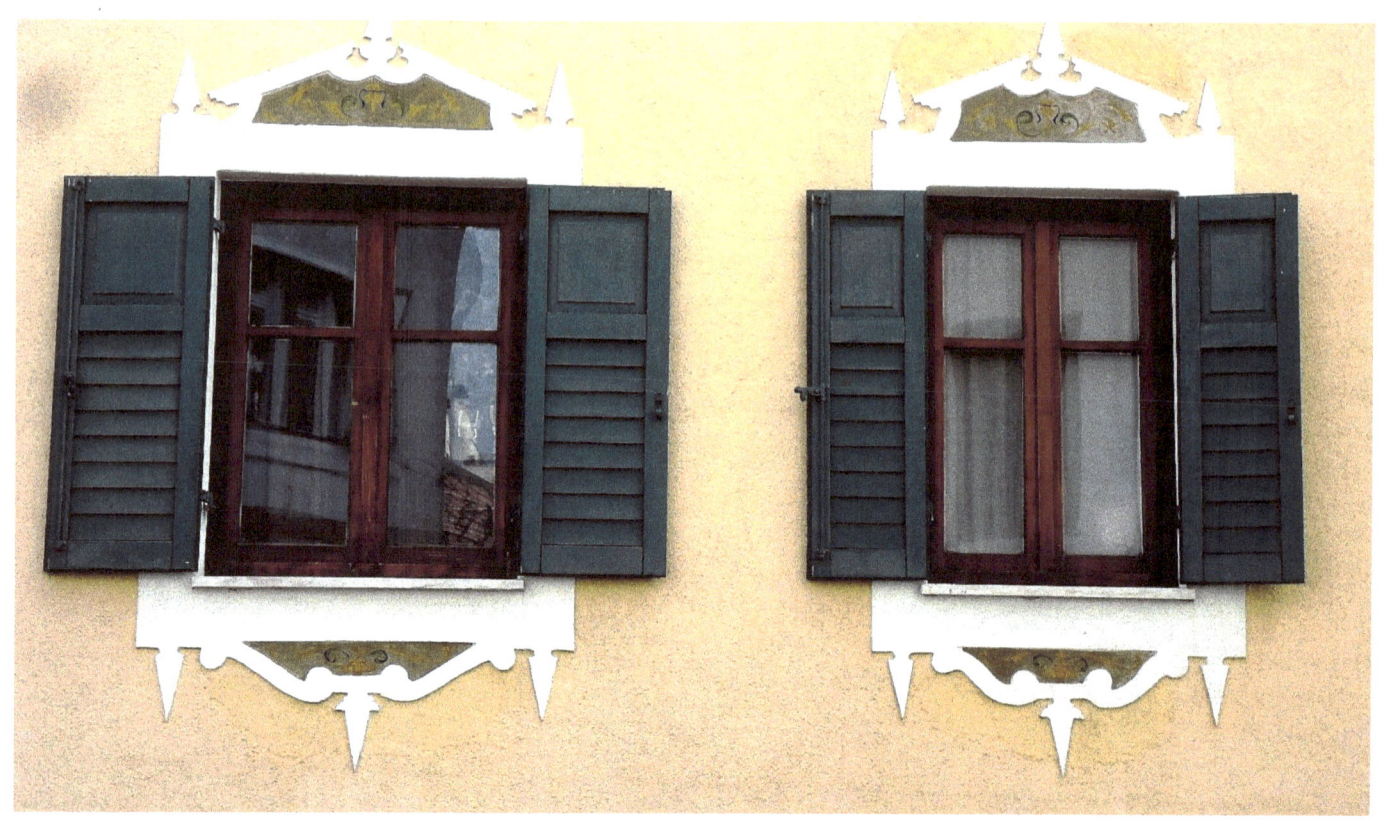

Vellutata di ortiche e borraggine, make a vegetable broth with half onion, mixed herbs (Swiss chard, spinach, borage, etc.), leek, carrot, celery, lovage, thyme, the hedgehog mushroom brown powder (sarcodon imbricatus). Brown in oil an onion and garlic finely chopped, then add the borage and nettles. Let wither and blend. Put in a pot again and just begins to boil put the flour, stirring constantly. Before it congeals add the hot broth adjusted with salt and bring to a boil for ten minutes. Whisk in a cup the egg yolk with Parmesan, join it to creamy soup and serve with croutons jumped in butter.

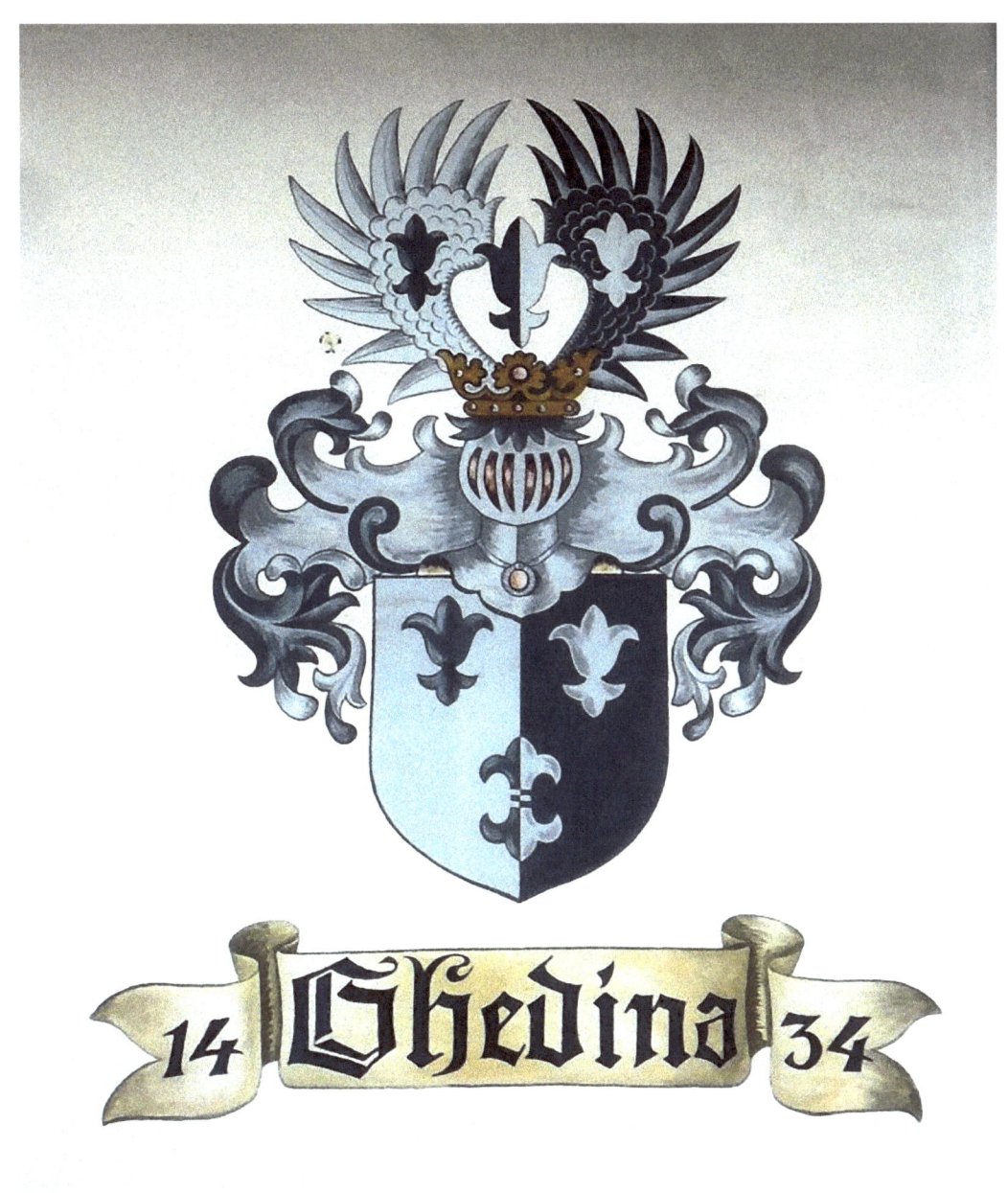

14 **Ghedina** 34

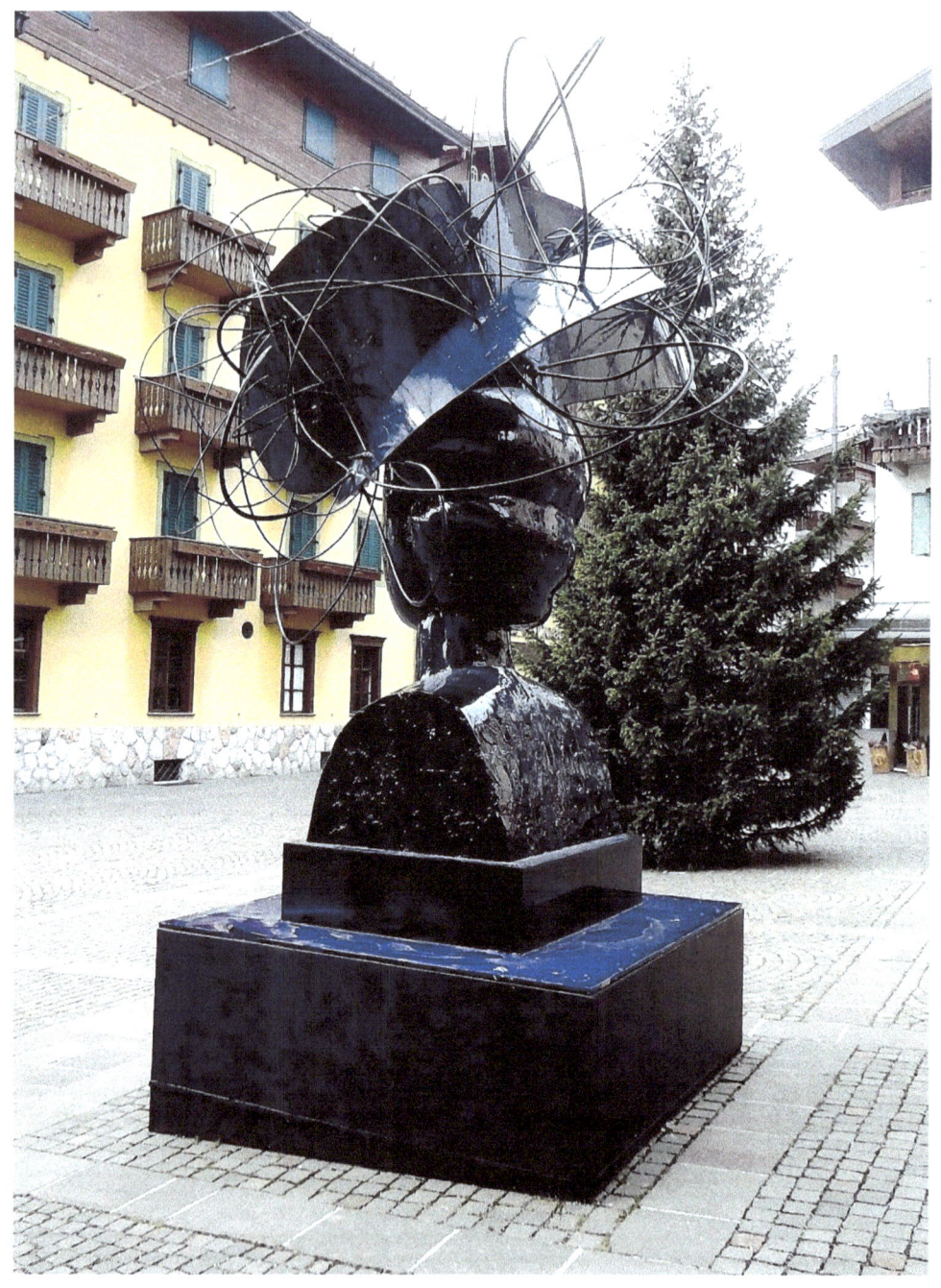

22

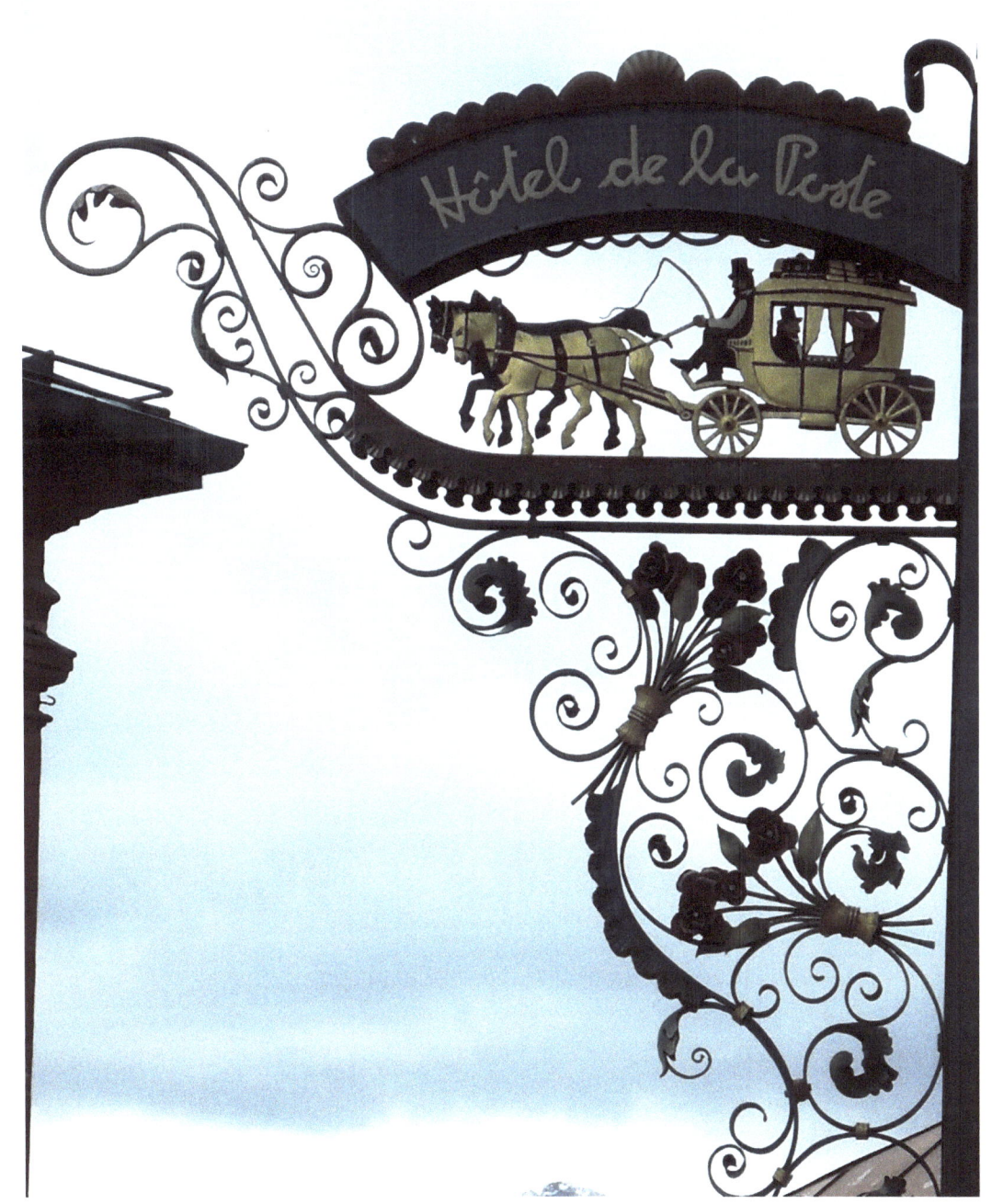

23

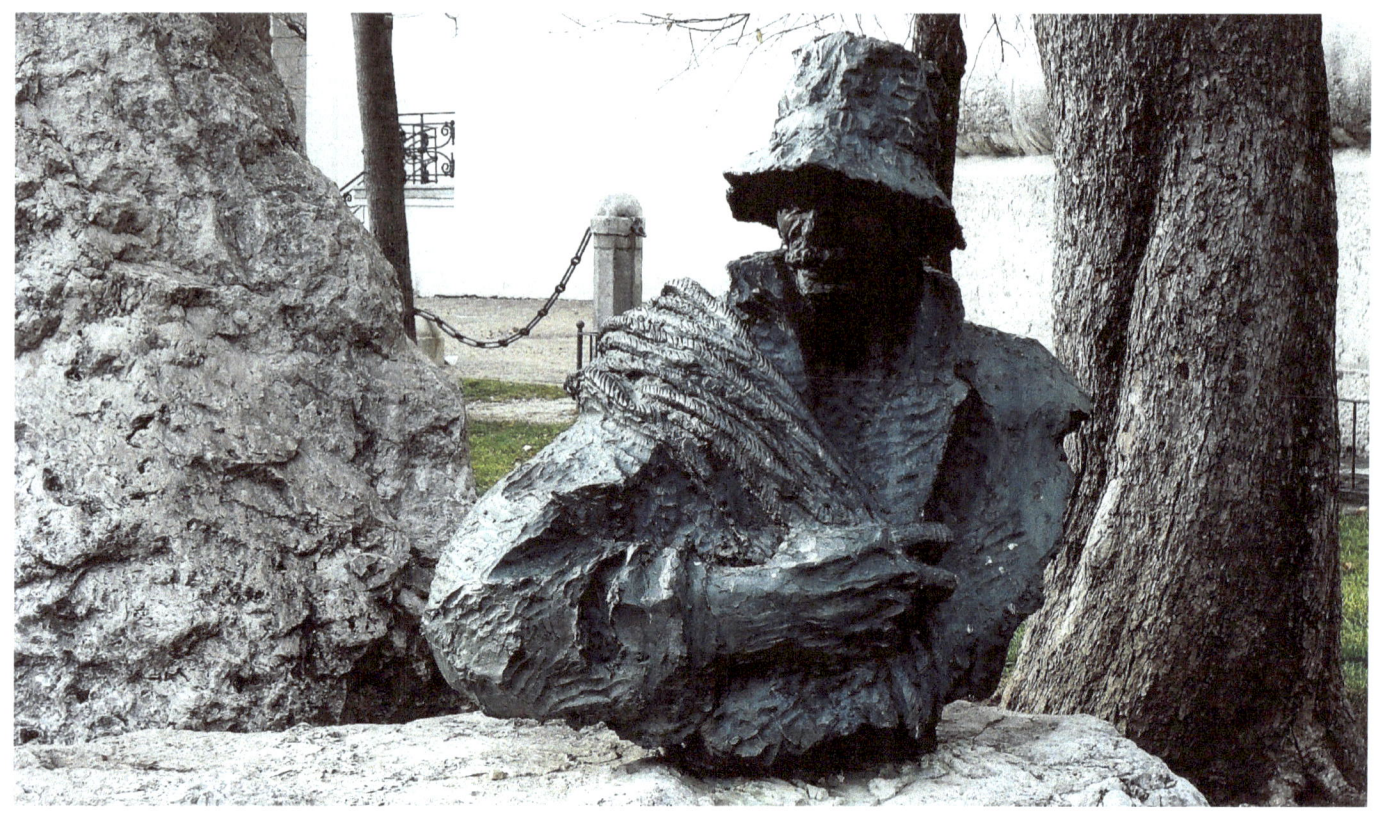

Arrosto in salsa di verdure stufate, in a pan put the sirloin meat tightly tied, butter, ham fat diced, salt, pepper and sear very well. Unite all the smells chopped (onion, celery, carrot, rosemary, black pepper) and let cook a few minutes on high heat. Add a ladleful at a time of vegetable stock and cook the meat on low heat for two hours. If necessary, add more broth to complete the cooking. Pass to mixer the stewed vegetables for a tasty cream. Cut the roast into slices and serve accompanied by the stewed vegetables sauce. If you like the smells, you can increase the amount, enriching even more the flavor of the roast.

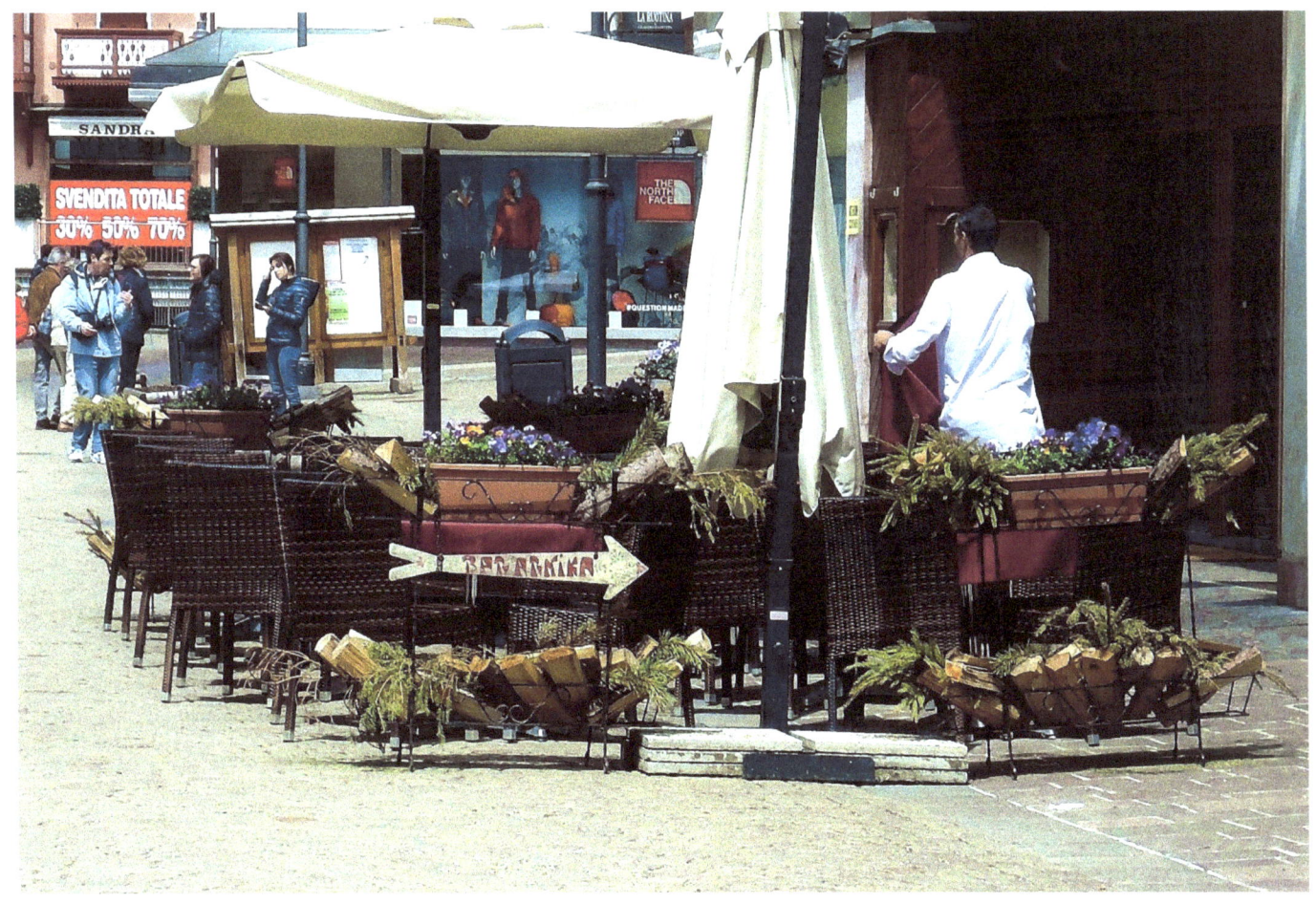

Capriolo in umido, cut the meat into pieces and let them marinate for a night with wine, celery, carrots, garlic, juniper berries, fennel seeds, the leaves of sage and laurel, rosemary, cinnamon and cloves. Drain the meat and brown in oil. Add the wine with herbs and spices and let evaporate. Continue cooking for about 3-4 hours. Completed the cooking, sift the bottom, adjust with salt and add the chopped parsley. Serve hot with the polenta.

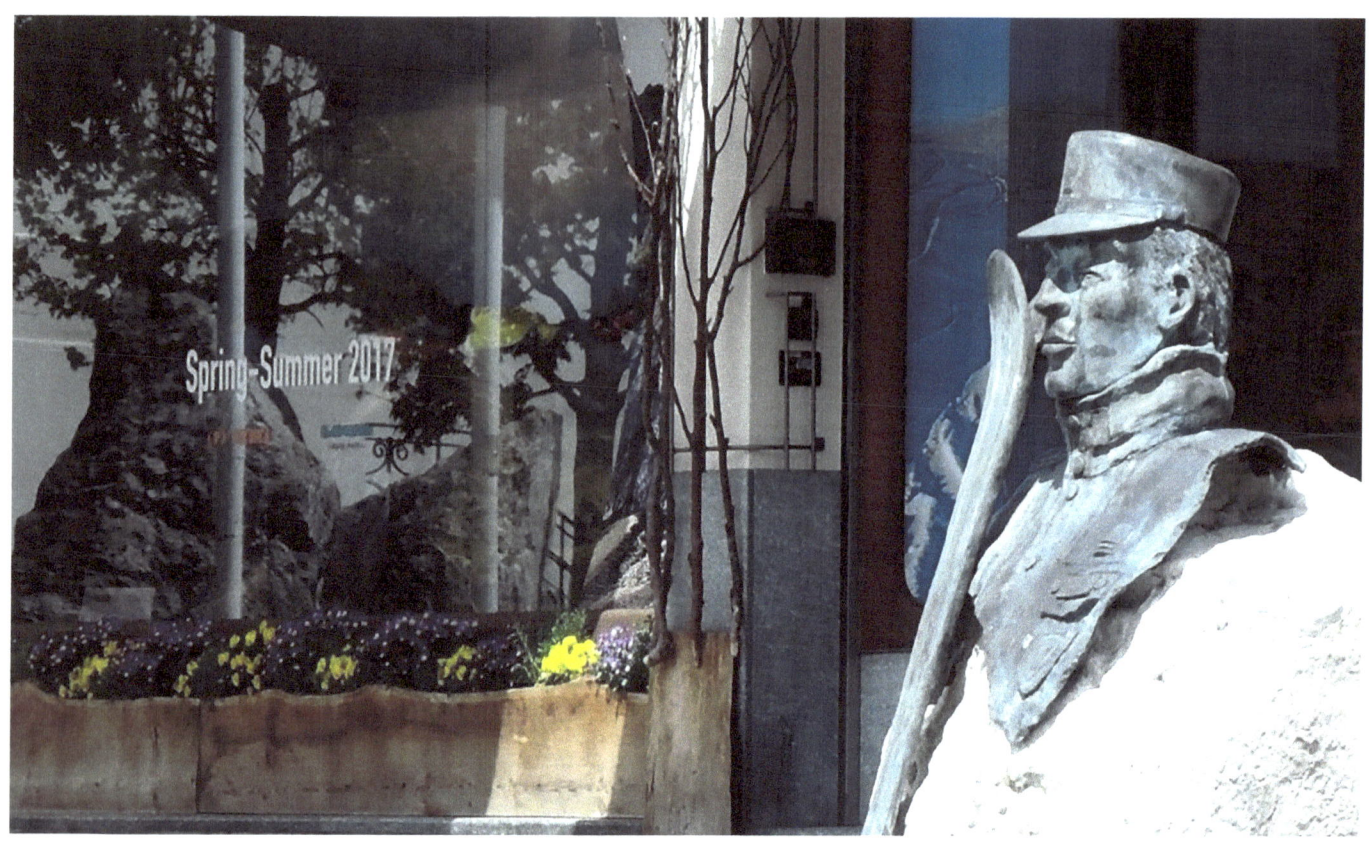

Costine di maiale con crauti e polenta, prepare a fried with olive oil, garlic, rosemary and sage, brown the spareribs (preferably smoked) and moisten with white wine. Separately prepare an onion bottom and bacon, add the sauerkraut, stew, add the spareribs and cook. Serve the sauerkraut with ribs and a slice of fuming polenta.

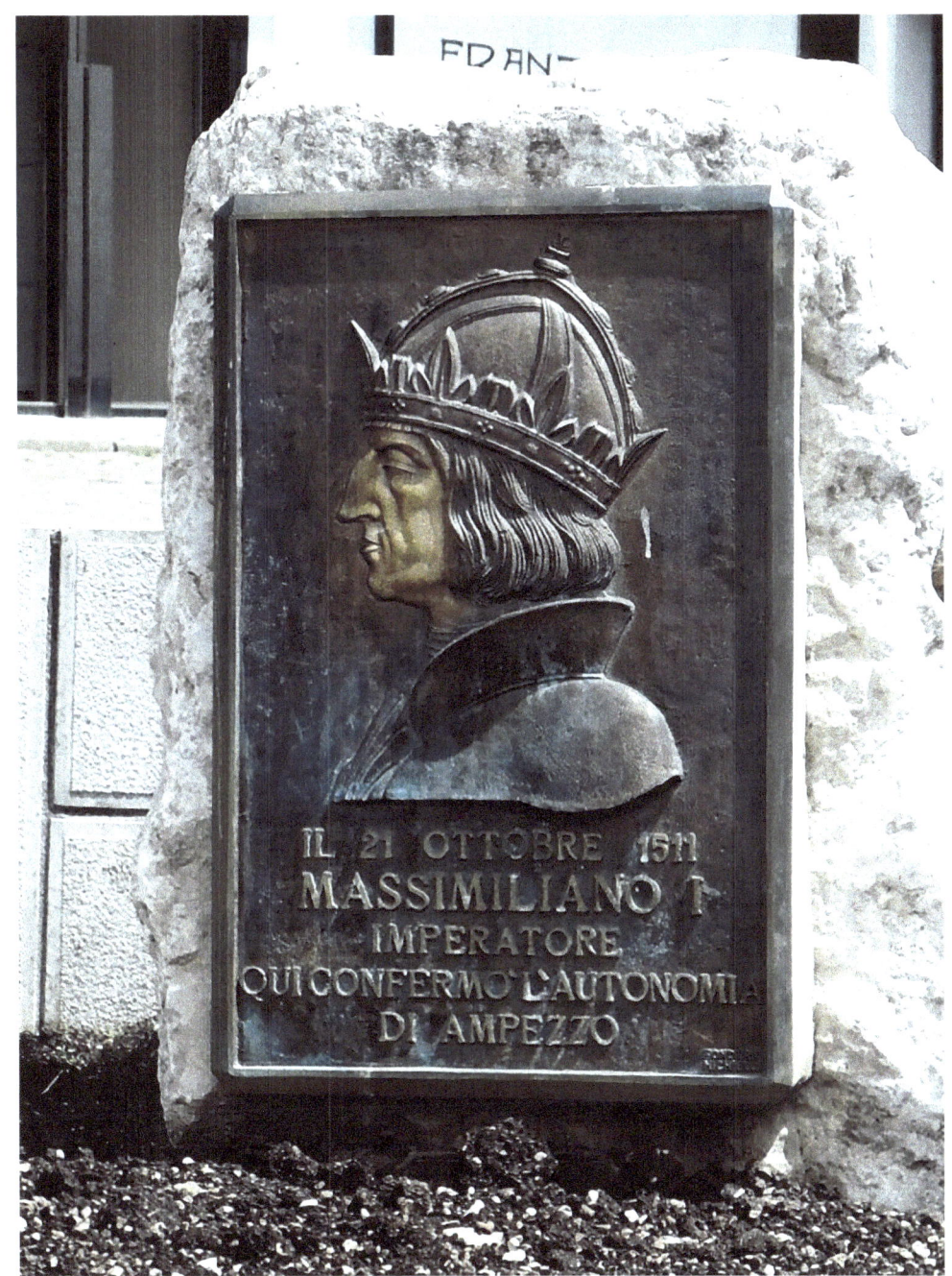

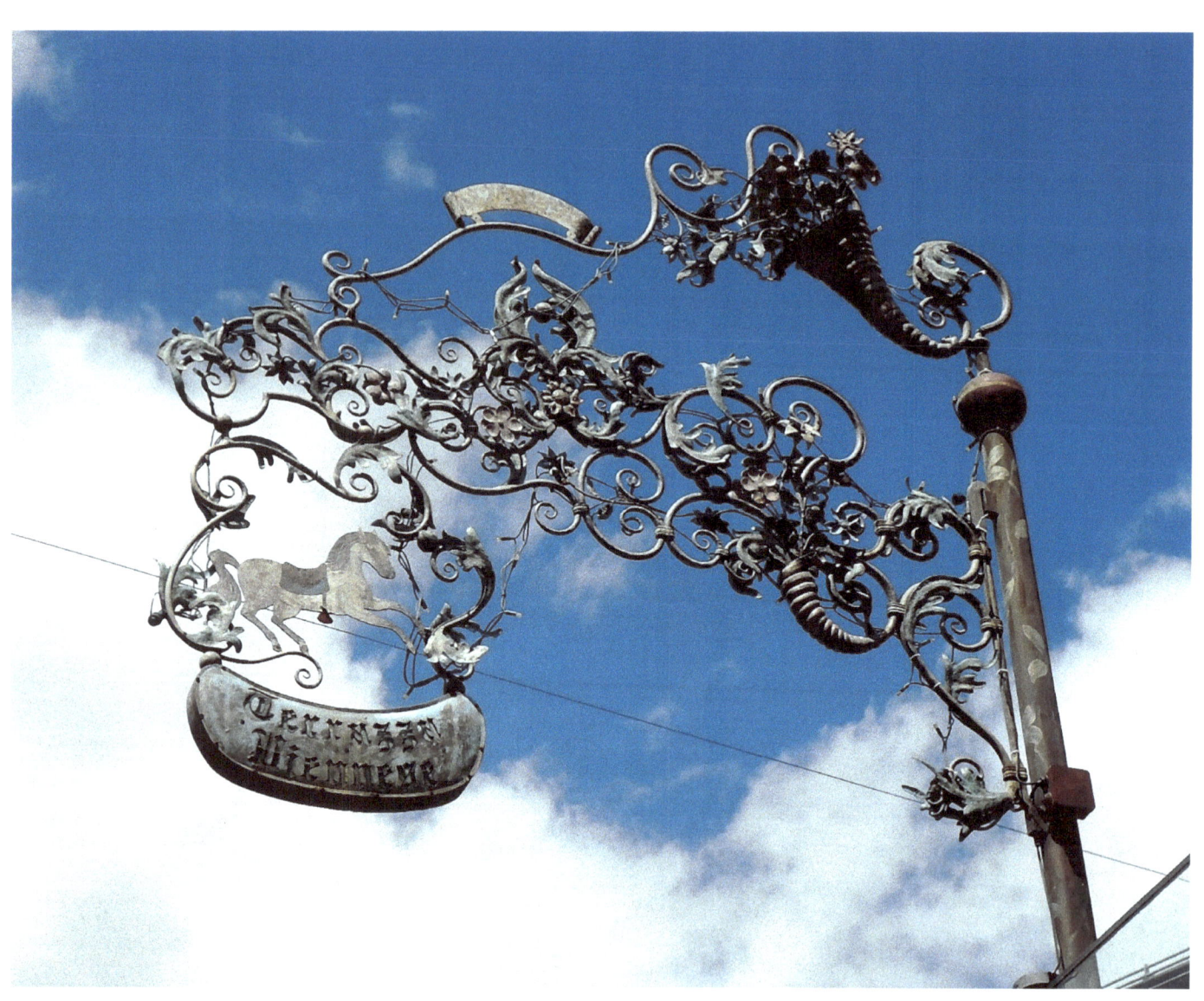

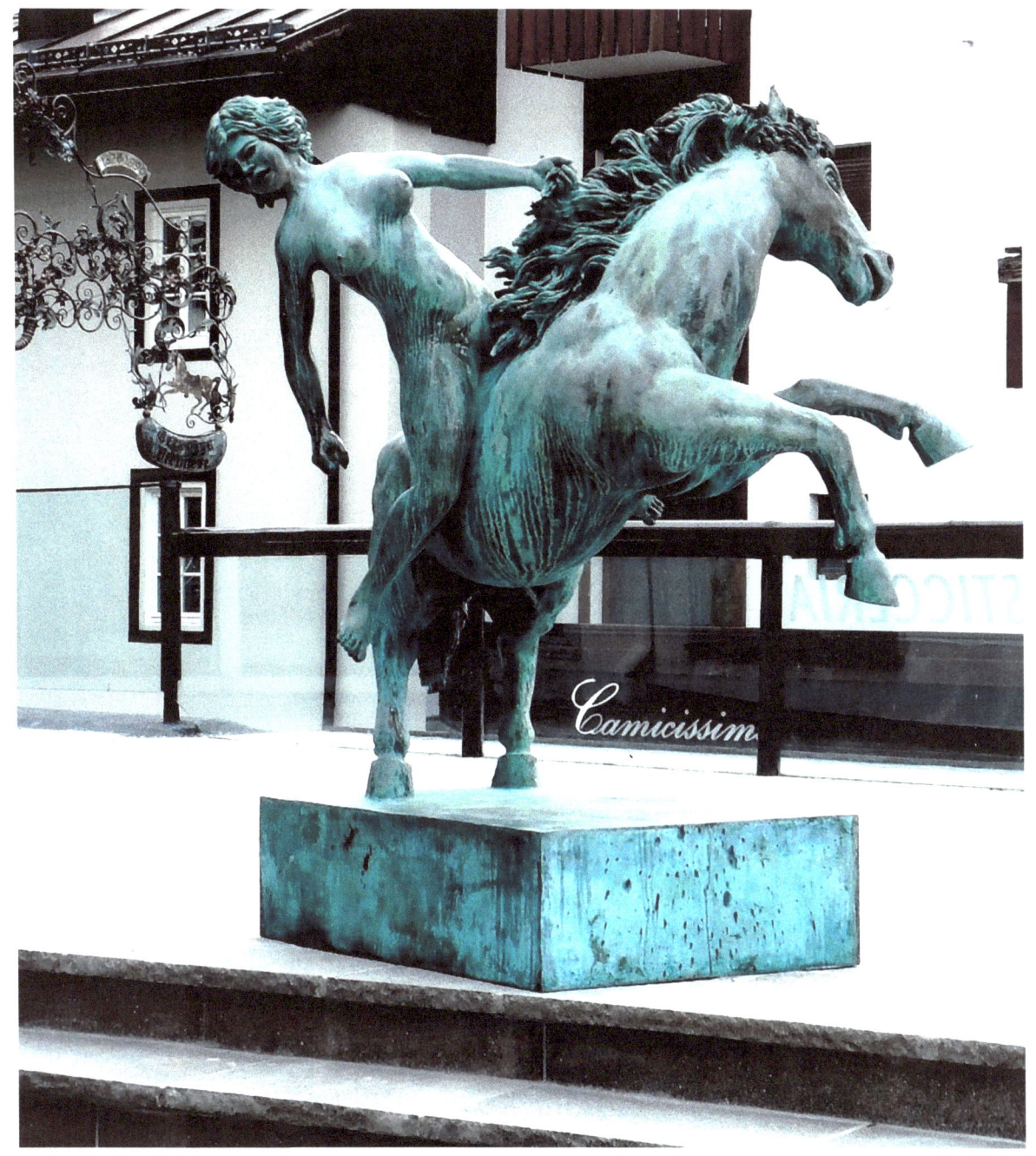

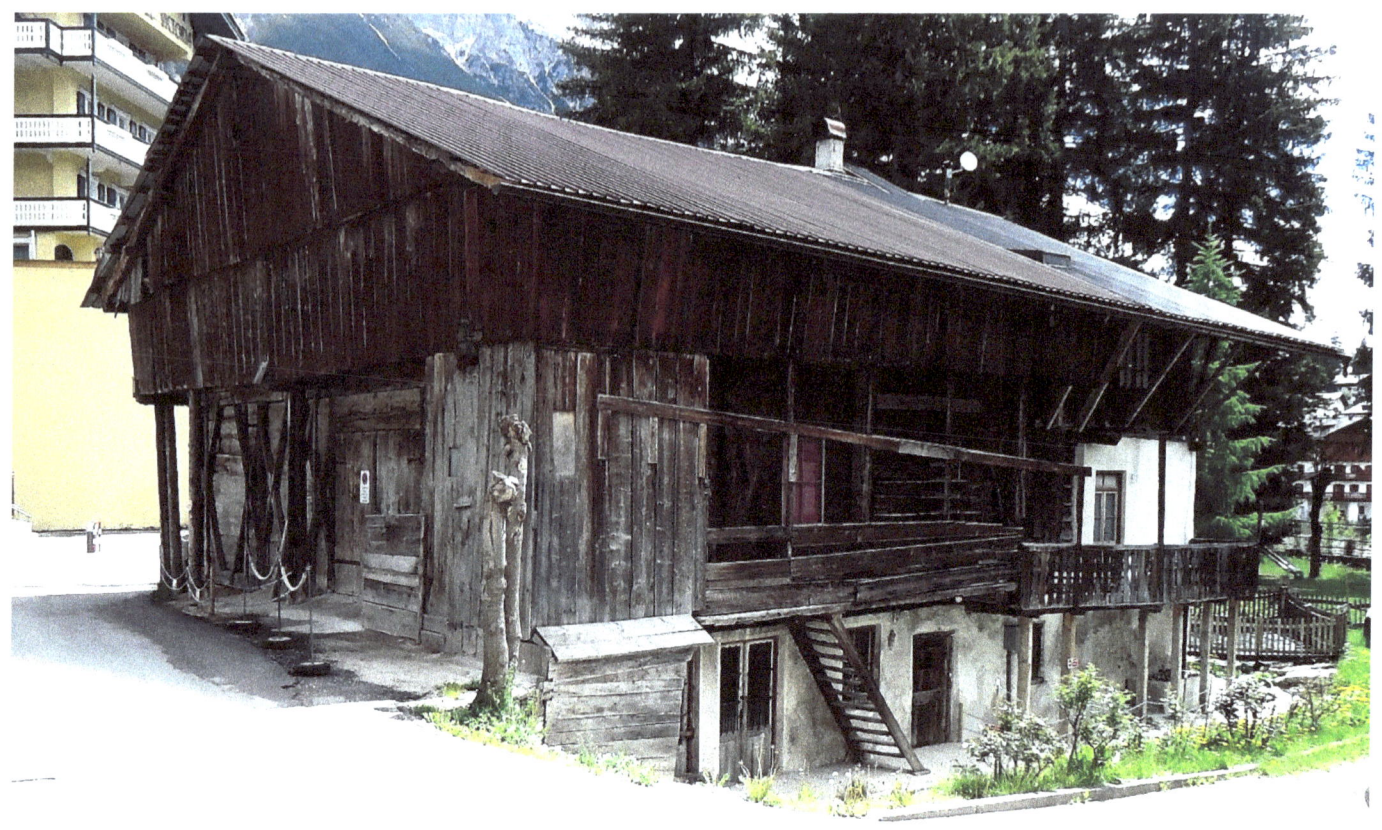

Maiale al latte, peel the onion and garlic, wash and dry the sage, bay leaf, the parsley stalks and celery. In a glass bowl, place the pork, add all the spices, onion, garlic and cover with vinegar and white wine. Wrap the bowl with a sheet of transparent film, place it in refrigerator and marinate for 24 hours, remembering to turn the meat occasionally. Let drain the meat from the marinade, pat dry and filter its liquid. In a saucepan, place the oil and the meat, bring to cooking for about three hours by lowering the flame. During cooking, add now and then the hot milk and the marinade, salt and pepper. When cooked, remove the meat from the pan and cut into slices. Place it in a dish and pour the sauce. Serve hot.

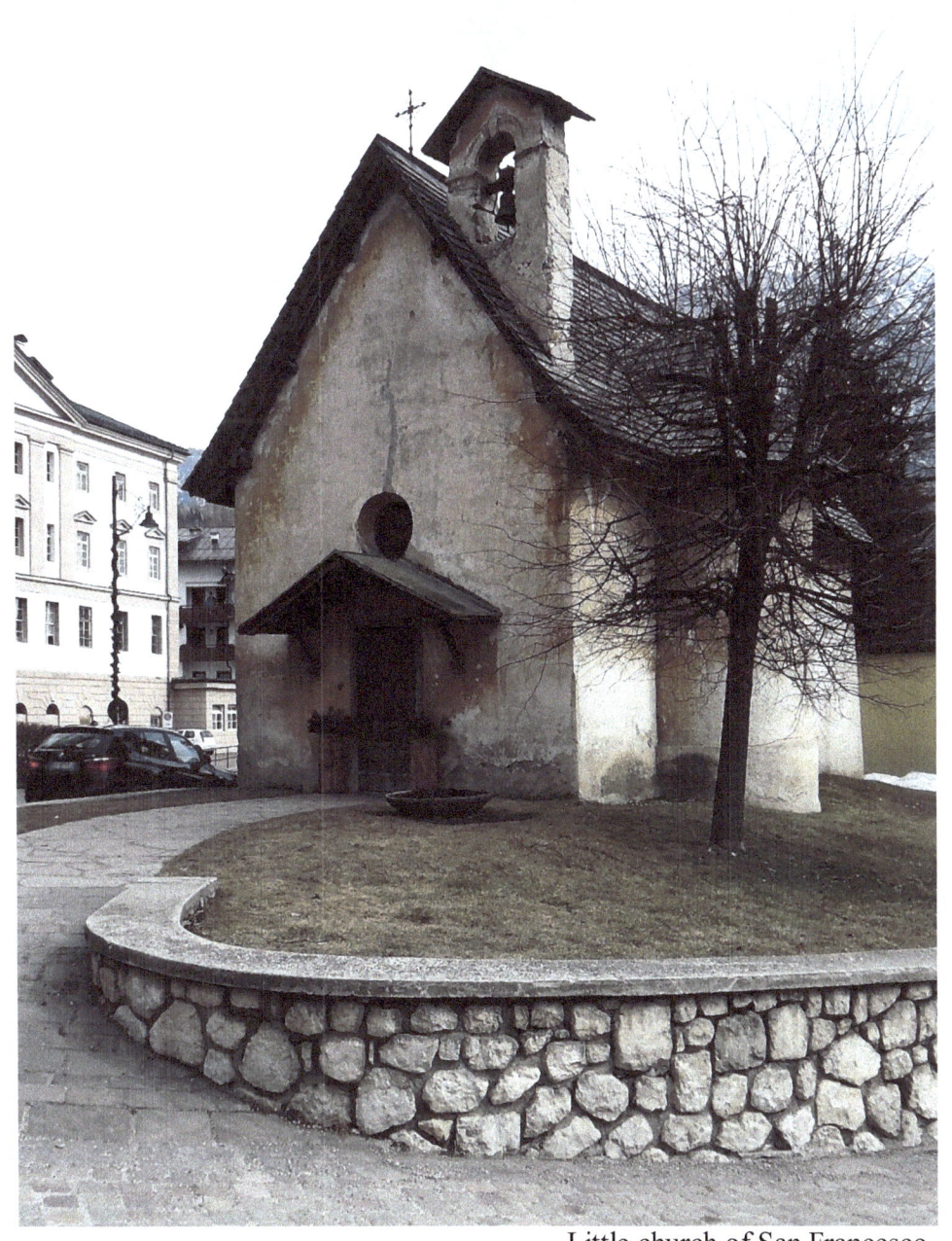

Little church of San Francesco

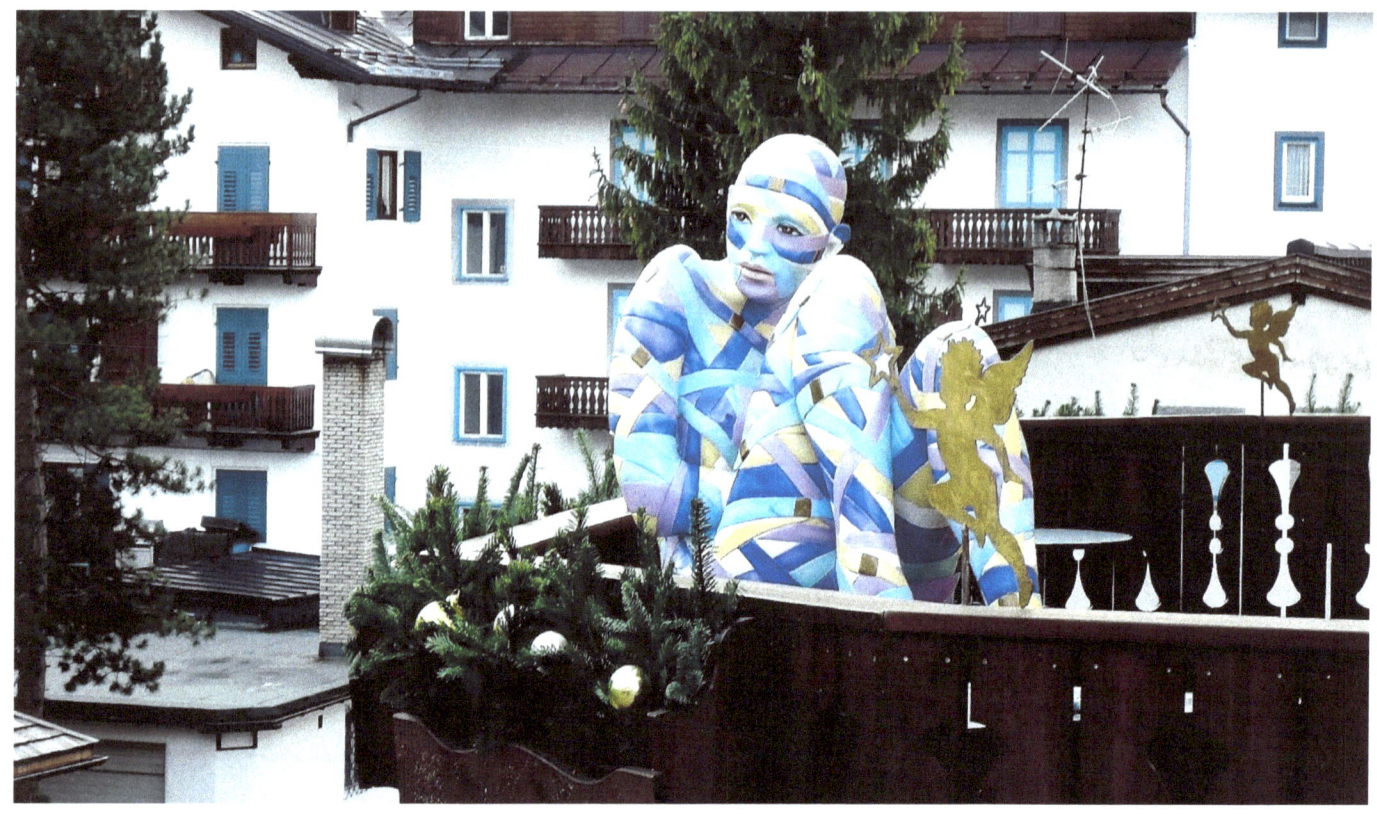

Pastin, typical dish of the Belluno province, made with fresh and spicy meat, but different from valley in valley and can be eaten raw or cooked. Utilize beef and pork together minced, season with olive oil, white wine, cinnamon, salt and a garlic and chopped bacon. Smear on slices of rustic bread or serve with polenta, or also mix it as a burger or a meatball and cooked on the grill.

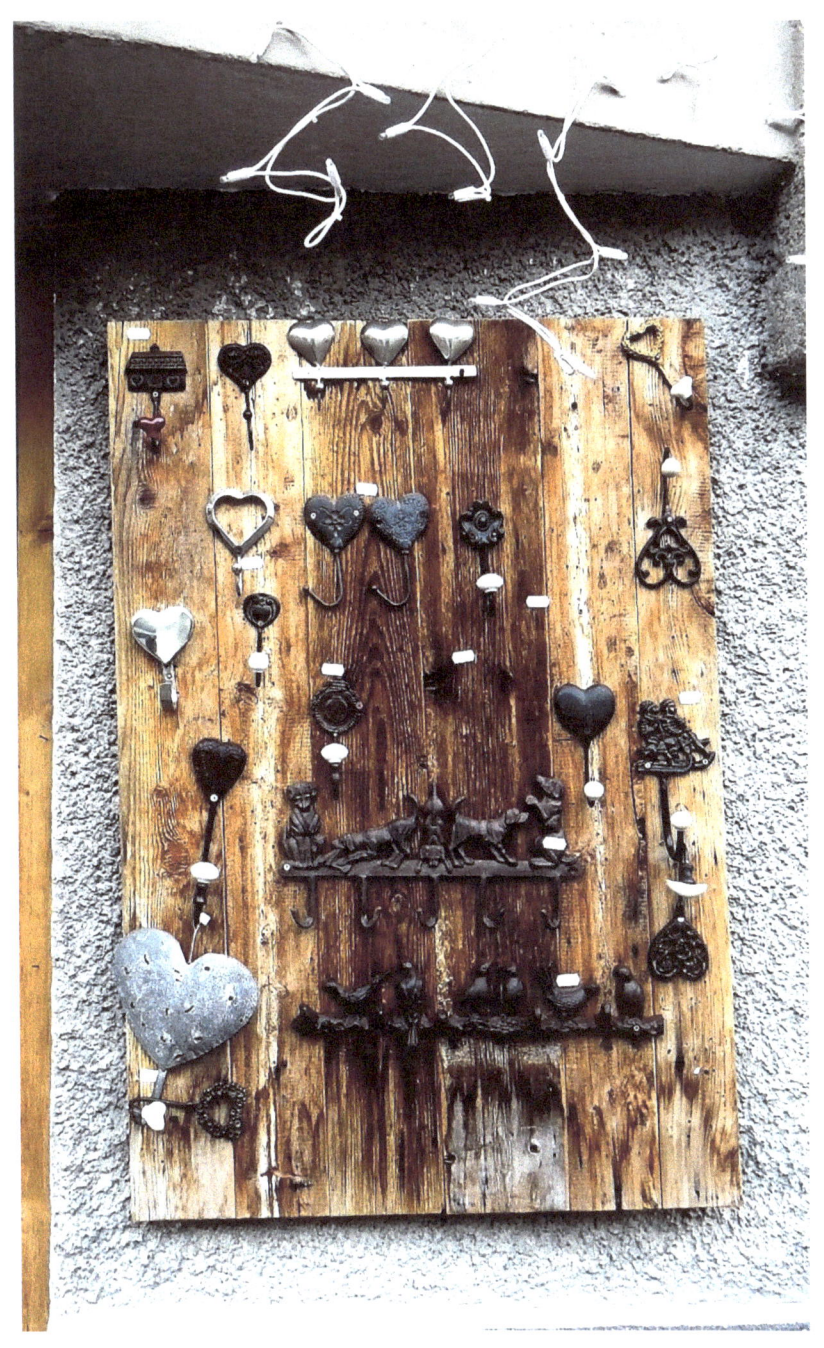

33

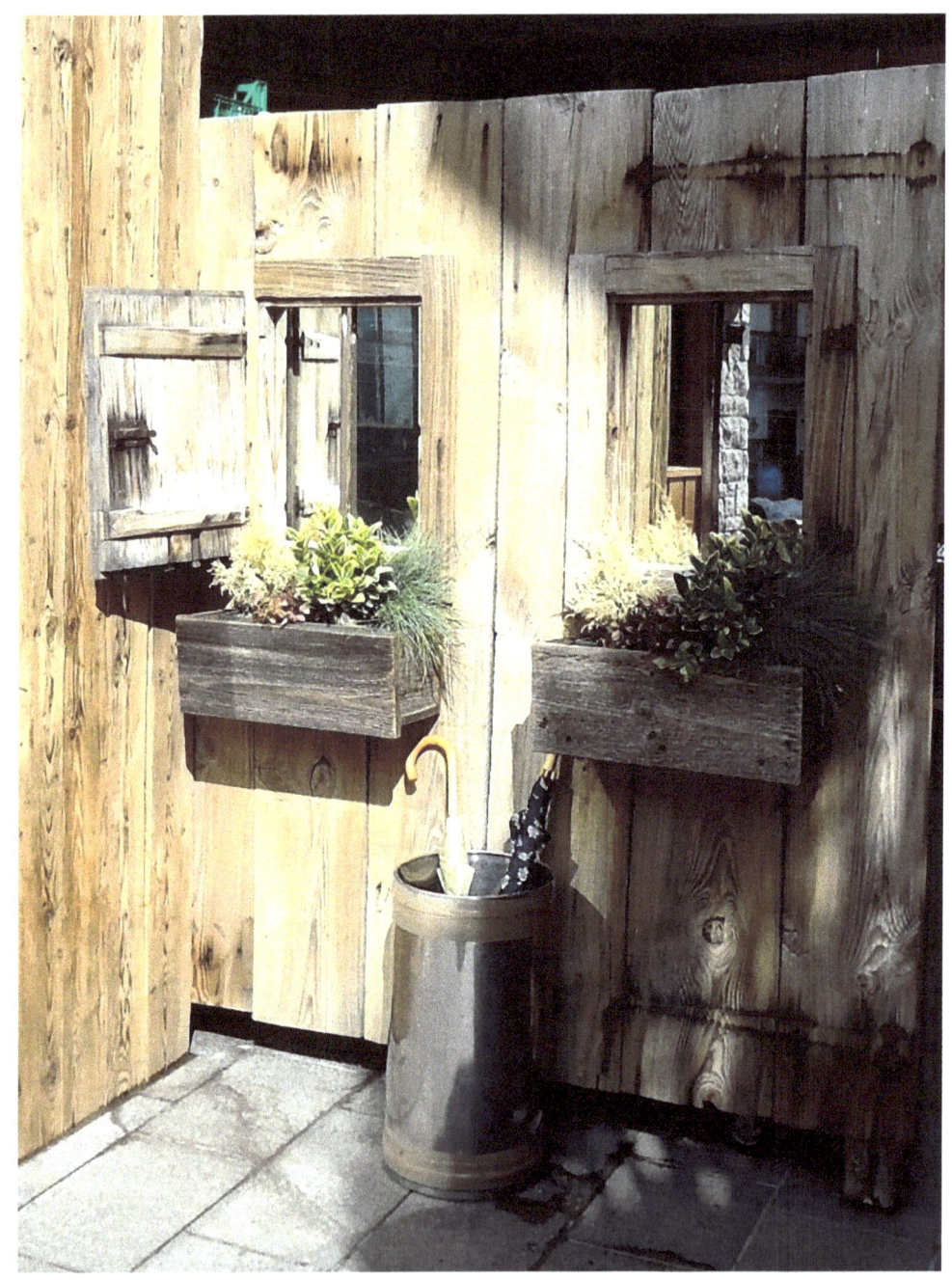

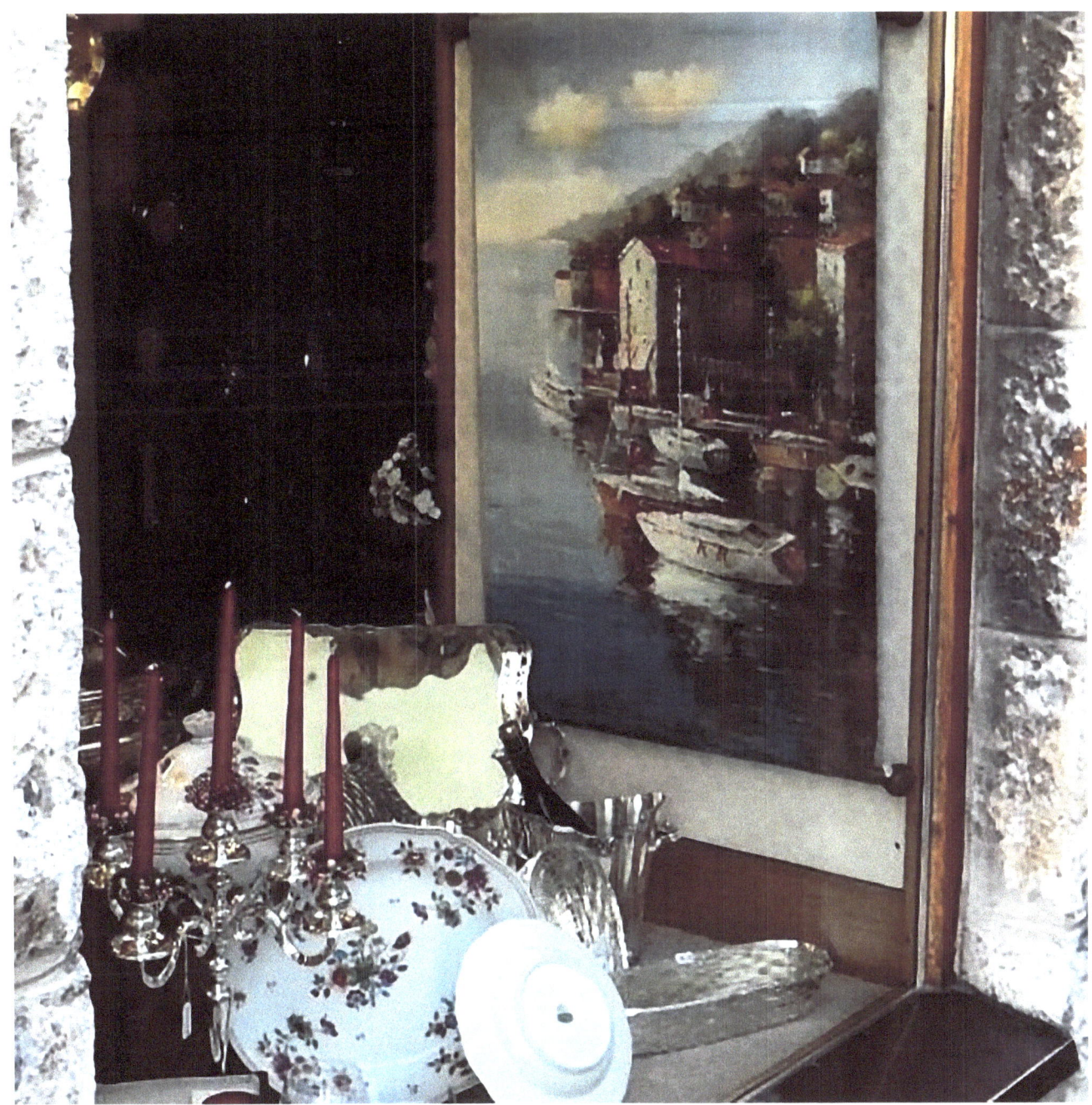

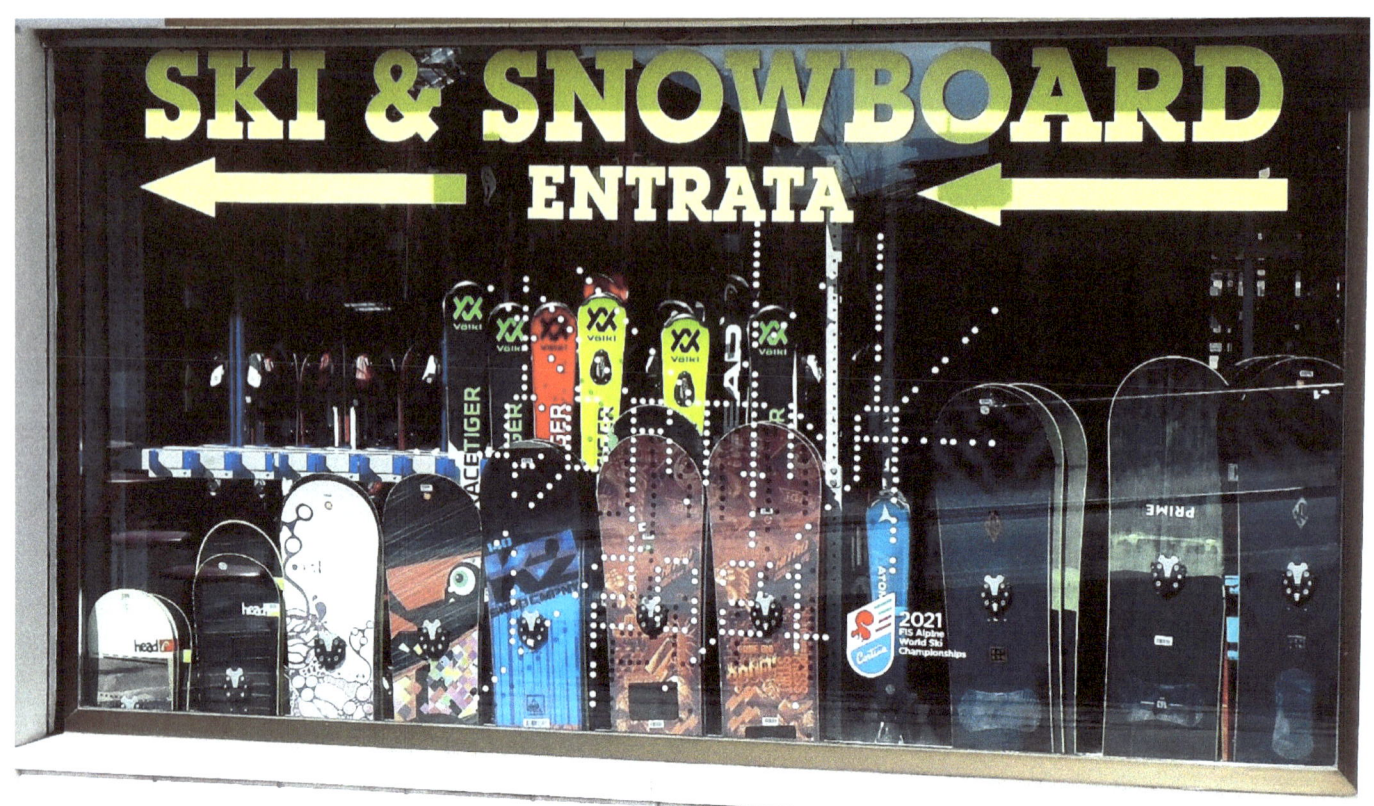

Pastissada de cavalo, beat the piece of meat to make it tender, then cut into pieces. Brown the sliced onion in oil and add the chopped tomatoes. Add salt and pepper, add the meat and cook for 20 minutes over medium heat. Pour the wine and let it dry. Cover the pan and cook over low heat for 3 hours. Serve piping hot with polenta.

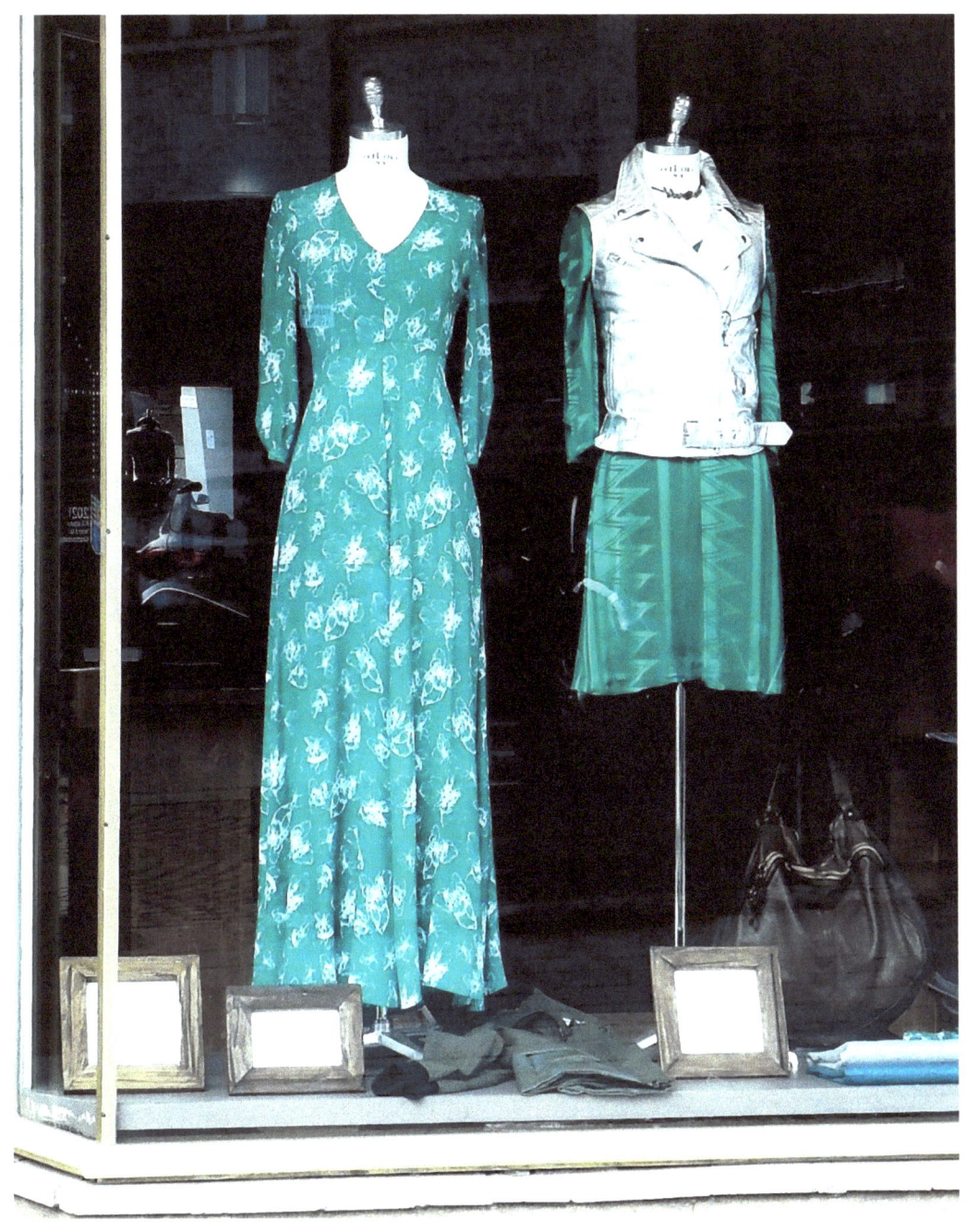

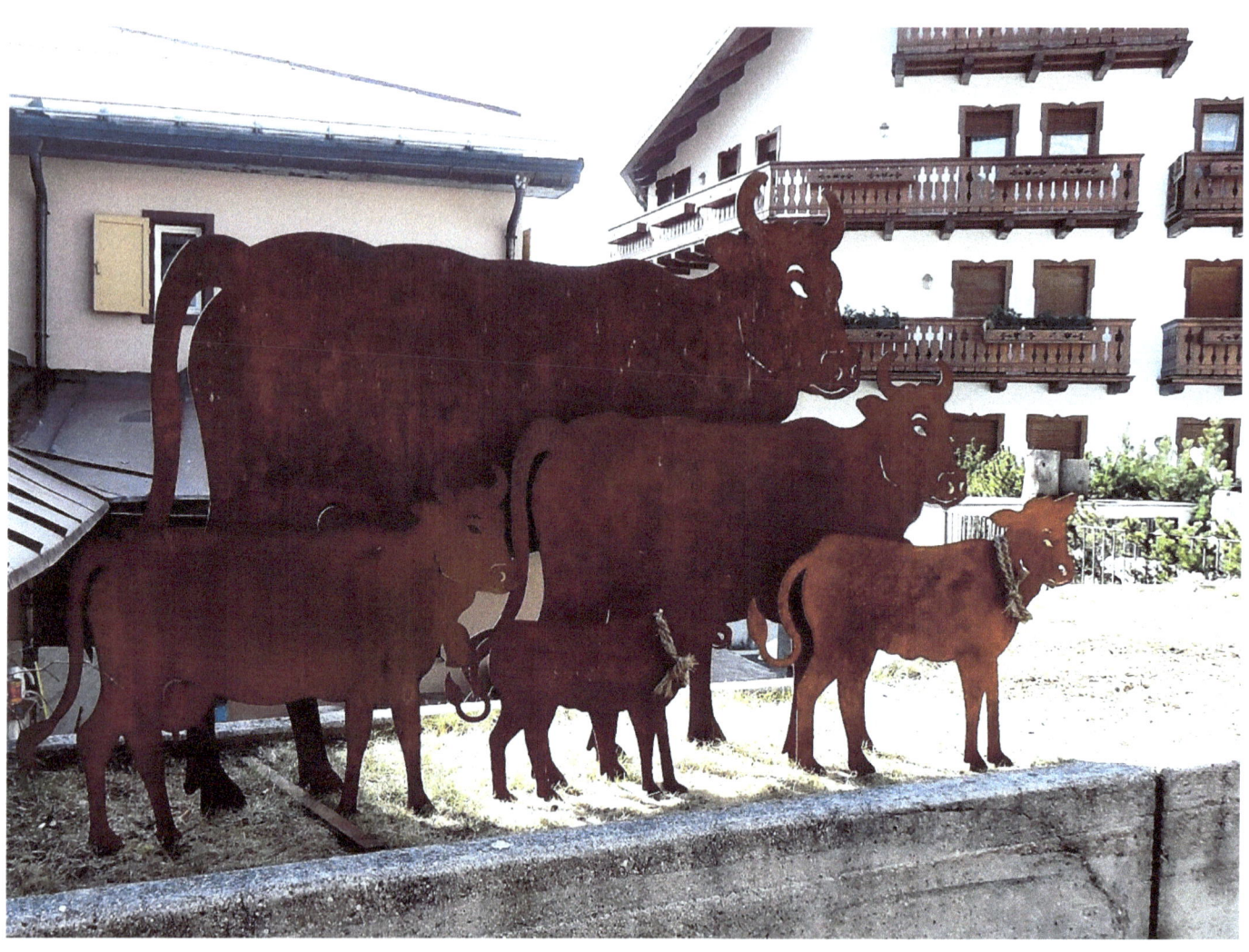

Péndole, they are thin strips of meat, long 15-20 cm, made to desiccate and smoke. The starting meat can be beef, pork, goat, but also horse or wild animals such as fallow deer that are left to soak for a few days with salt, pepper, red wine, a pinch of cinnamon, rosemary, sage and garlic or in juniper. The smoking techniques are at least two: the first consists in hanging the strips in infix nails in wooden rods at a distance of 2-3 cm from each other, the second in inserting the meat portions into iron rods (as if they were knitting needles) of 2-3 mm size...

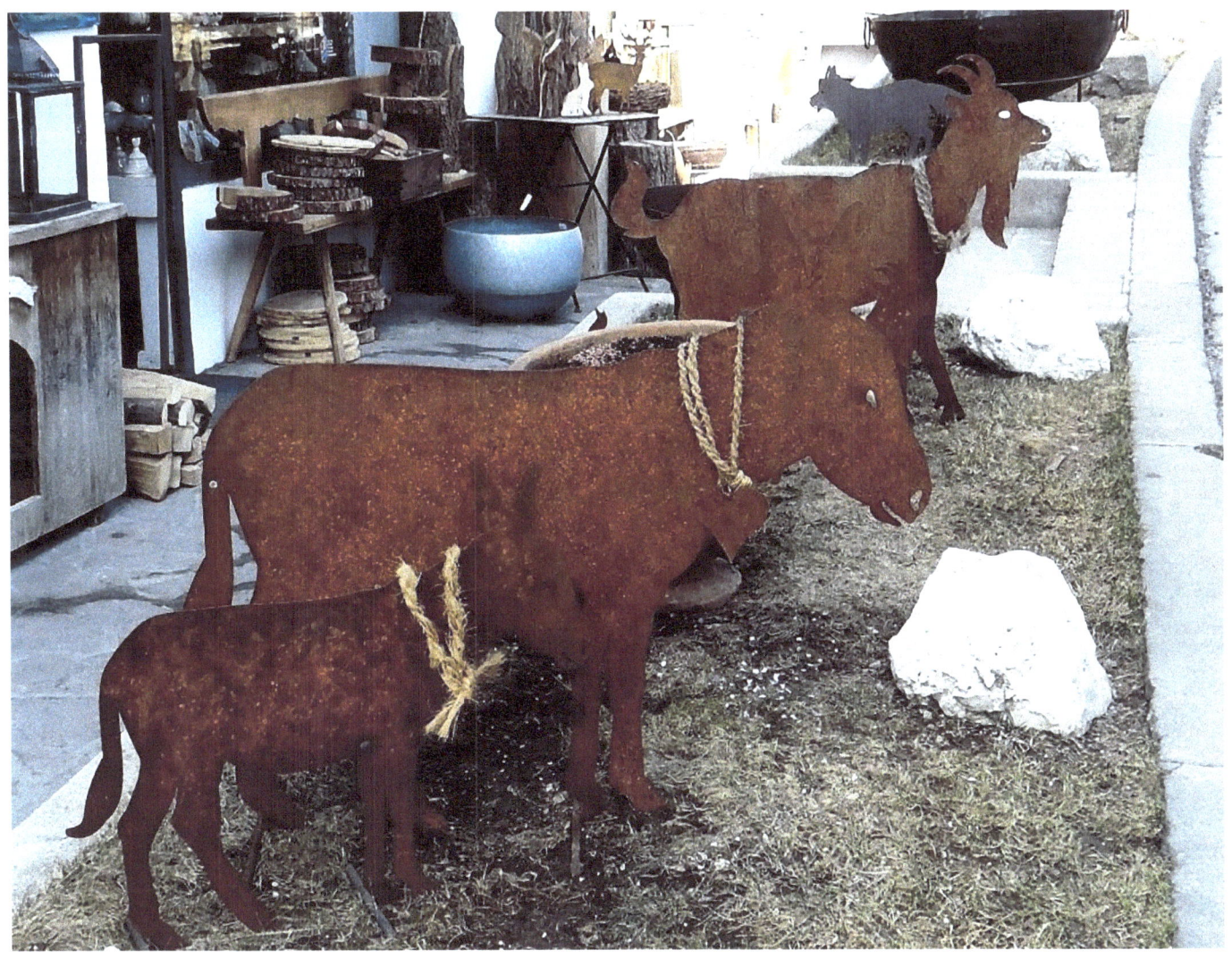

...At this point they are exposed to a cold smoke generated from sawdust of hard and white woods, such as beech and hornbeam. On the floor of the smoking process room it interposes between these two layers one of sawdust of juniper fronds and lights a small fire slowly burning generating full-bodied volutes of aromatic smoke that envelop the péndole. Generally they serve six to seven days to reach optimum drying. The anatomical parts utilized for the swine are the neck, the shoulder and the thigh, while for adult cattle it is utilized the haunch and other cuts to long fiber.

39

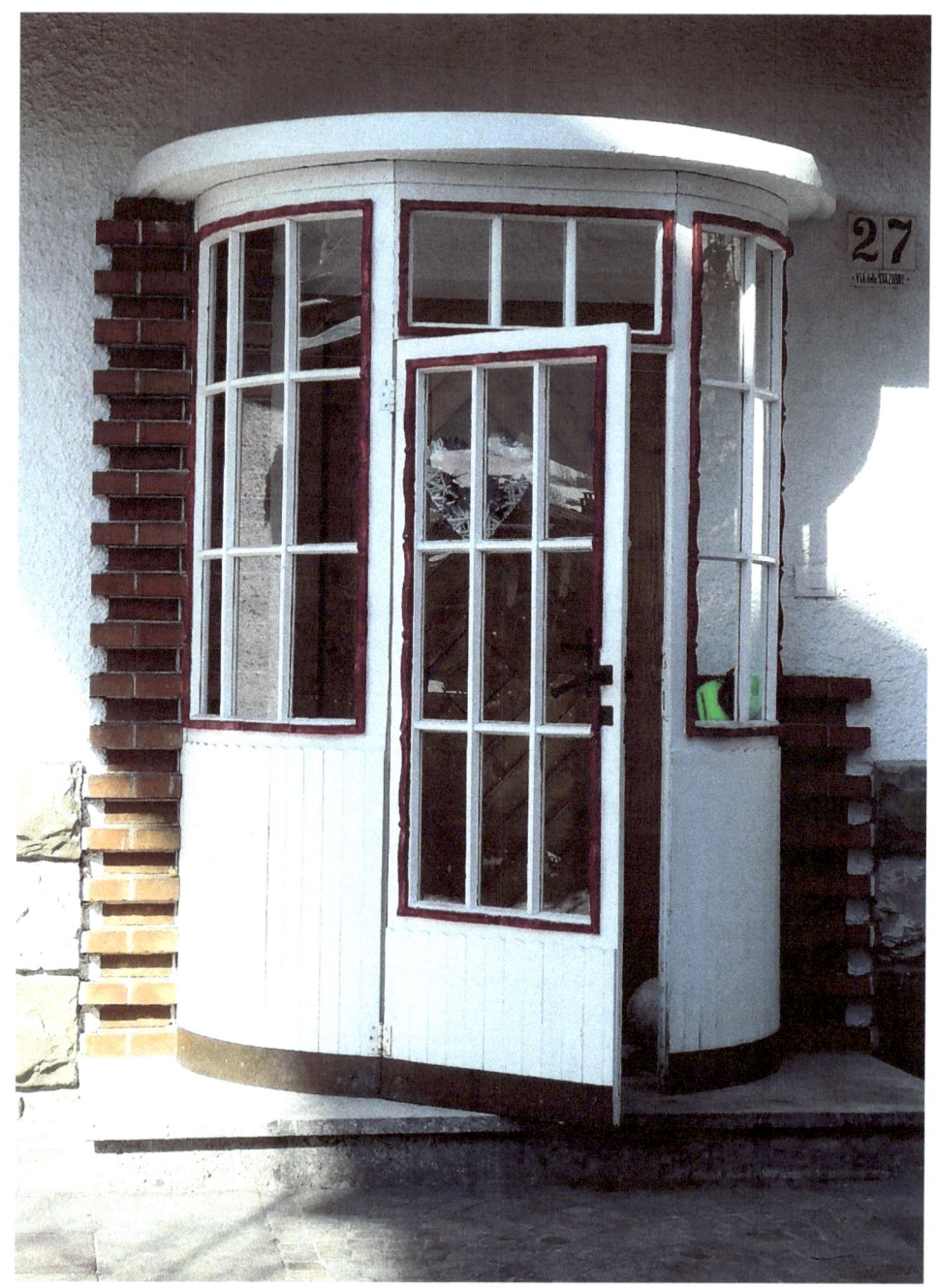

40

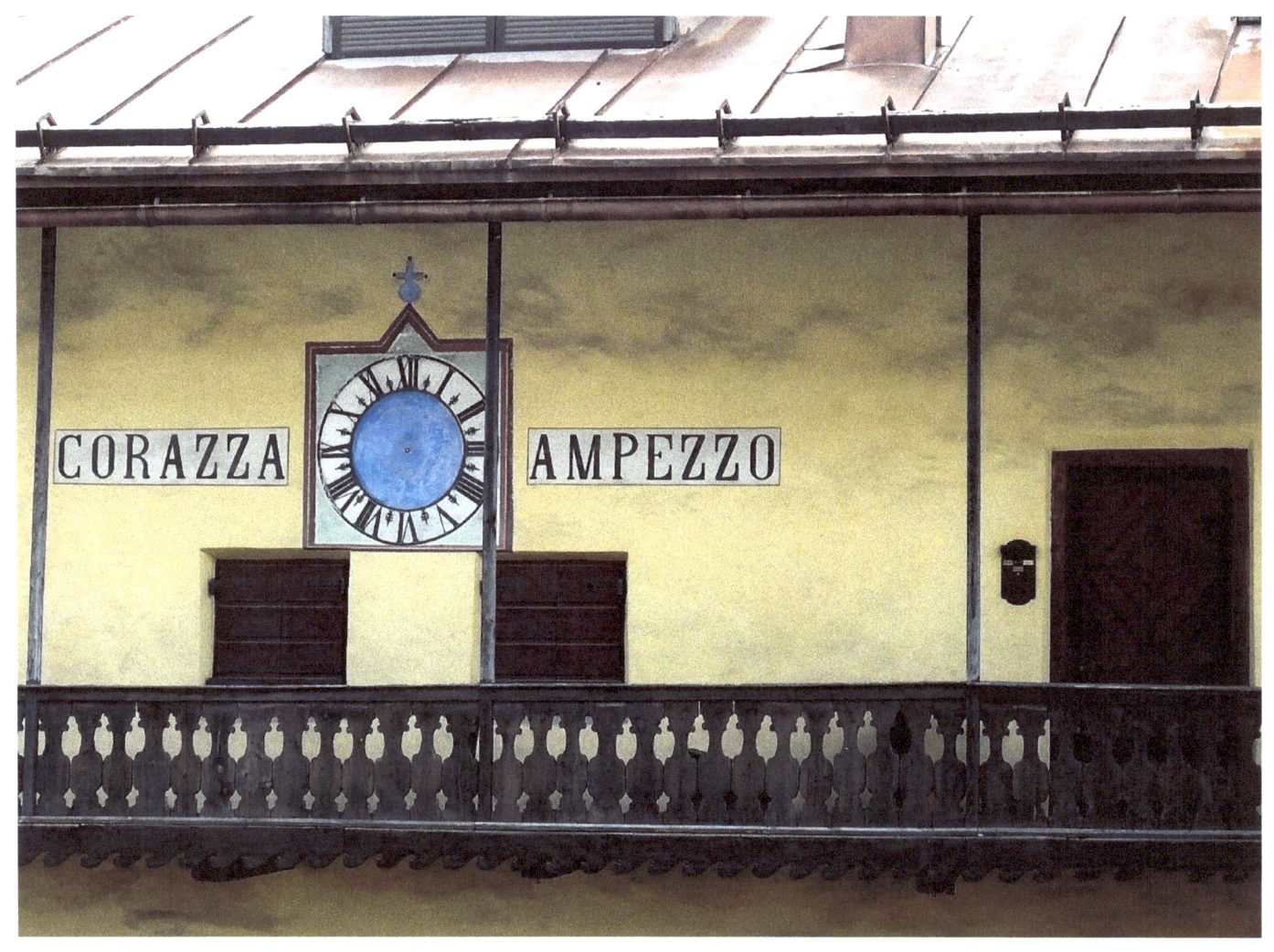

Spezzatino di cervo, Veneto dish made with venison. It is flesh with a slightly wild flavor, which is matured long time and then marinated in spiced wine. It is cooked on moist, with very slow cooking to soften the taste of game without sacrificing its softness.

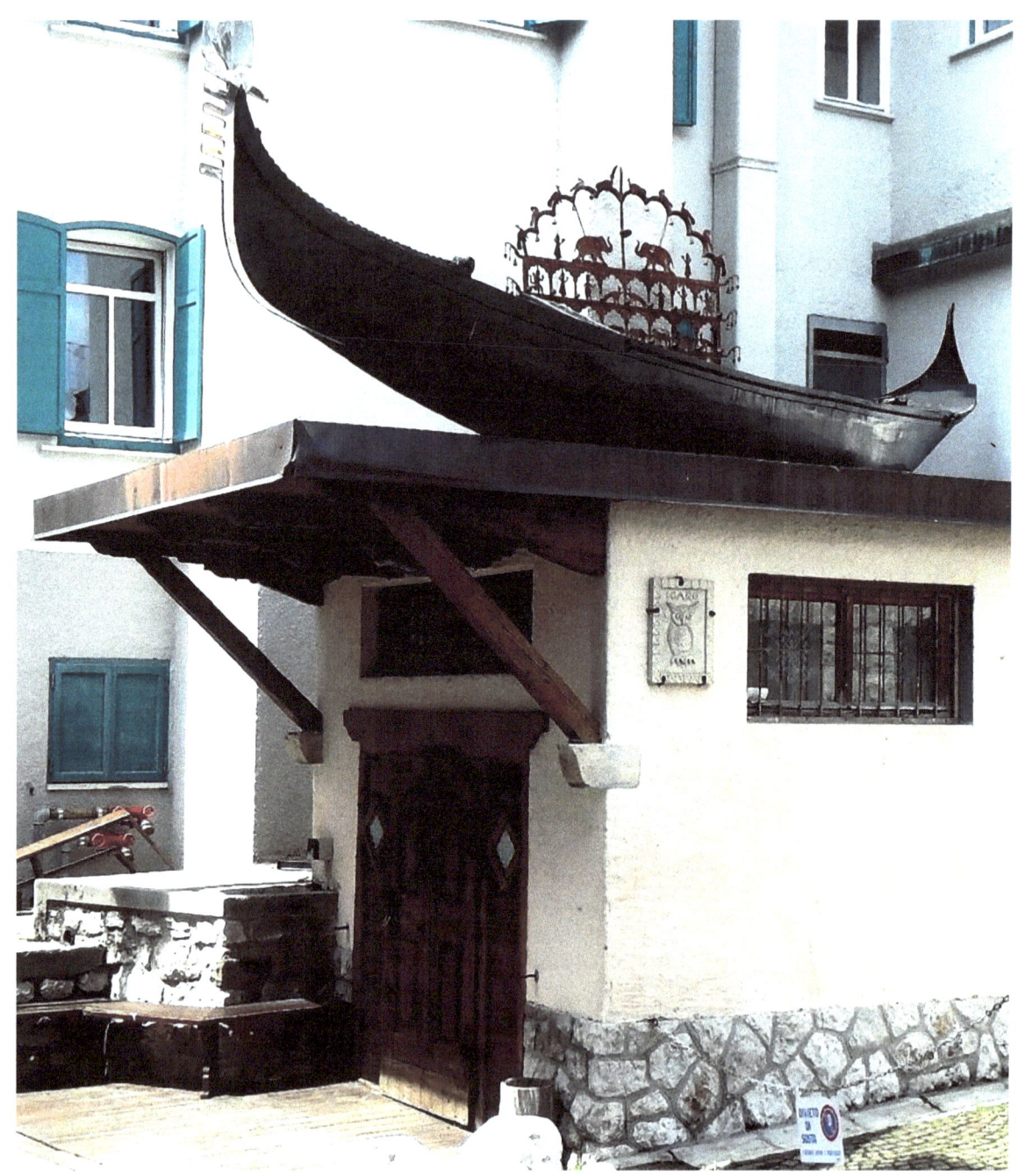

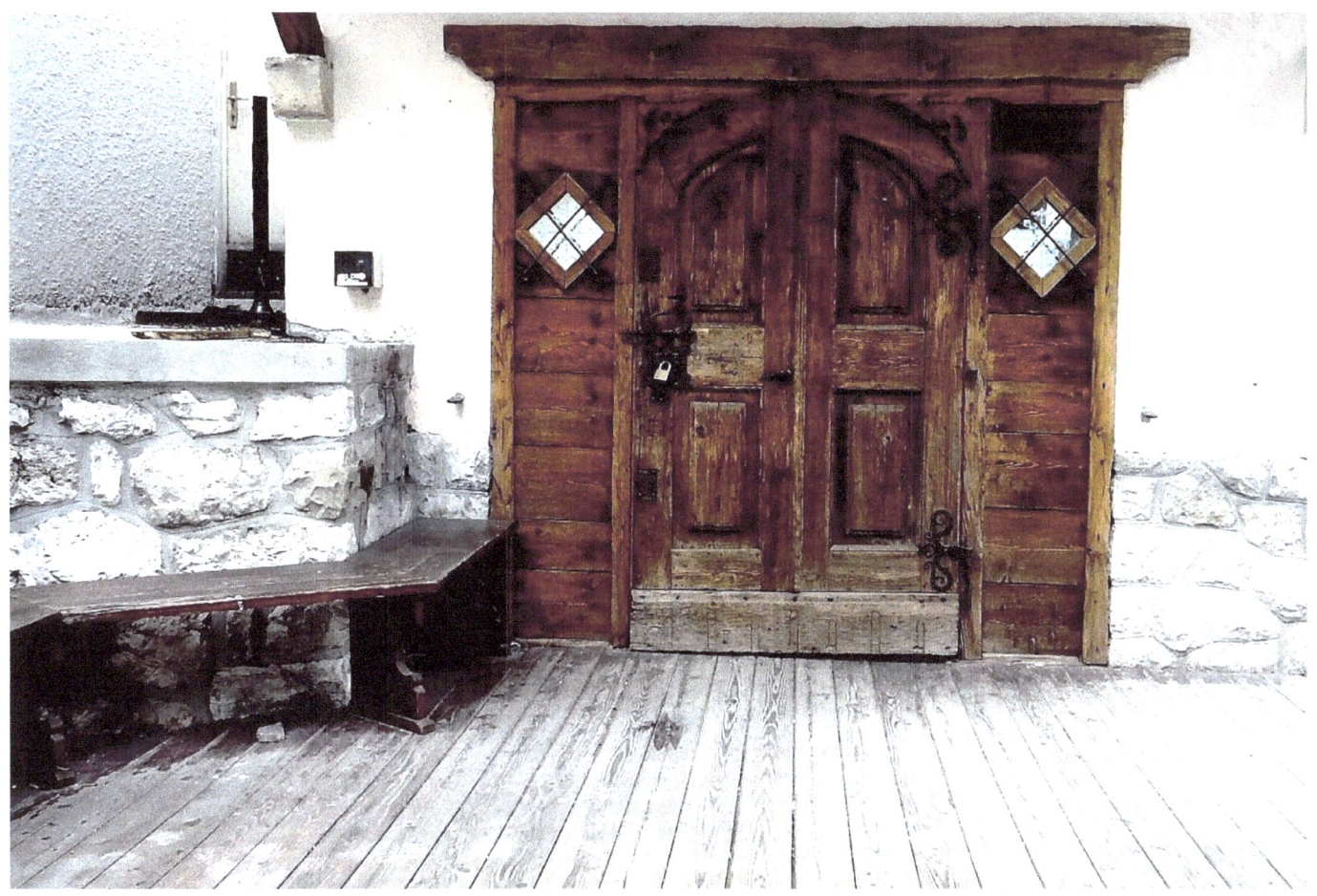

Finferli e funghi porcini, stewed, roasted, in sauce or as a side dish, the prized ceps and the tasty chanterelles are proposed by the local cuisine in countless variations.

Formaggi di malga, from them it gets the Frico, a typical very tasty dish. The cheese is melted in a pan with the butter until it forms a sort of omelette which can be served with polenta or with boiled potatoes, diced. In addition to the alpine cheese you can also use the montasio.

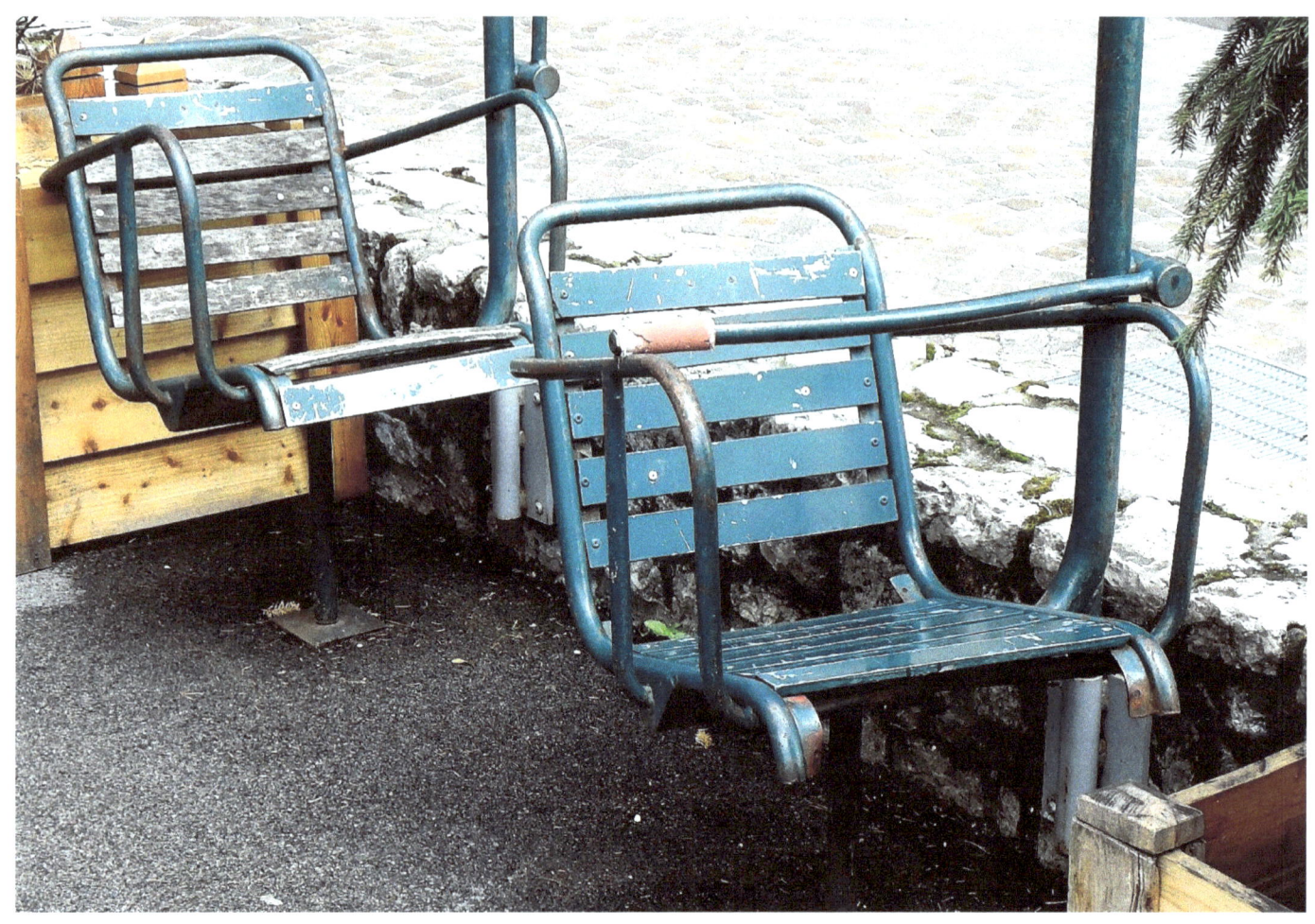

Patate all'ampezzana. Boil the potatoes with the peel (possibly in a pressure cooker to shorten the time: 15'), cool them, peel and cut them into large pieces. In a non-stick pan, brown the speck cut into strips with a little oil for 5 minutes. Remove the speck and set it aside in a bowl. In the same pan, sauté the thinly sliced onions with a little oil until they fade. Add the potatoes, add salt, sprinkle with rosemary and cook over low heat for 20-30 minutes, stirring occasionally. Halfway through cooking, add the speck too. In the end they must be a little bit broken.

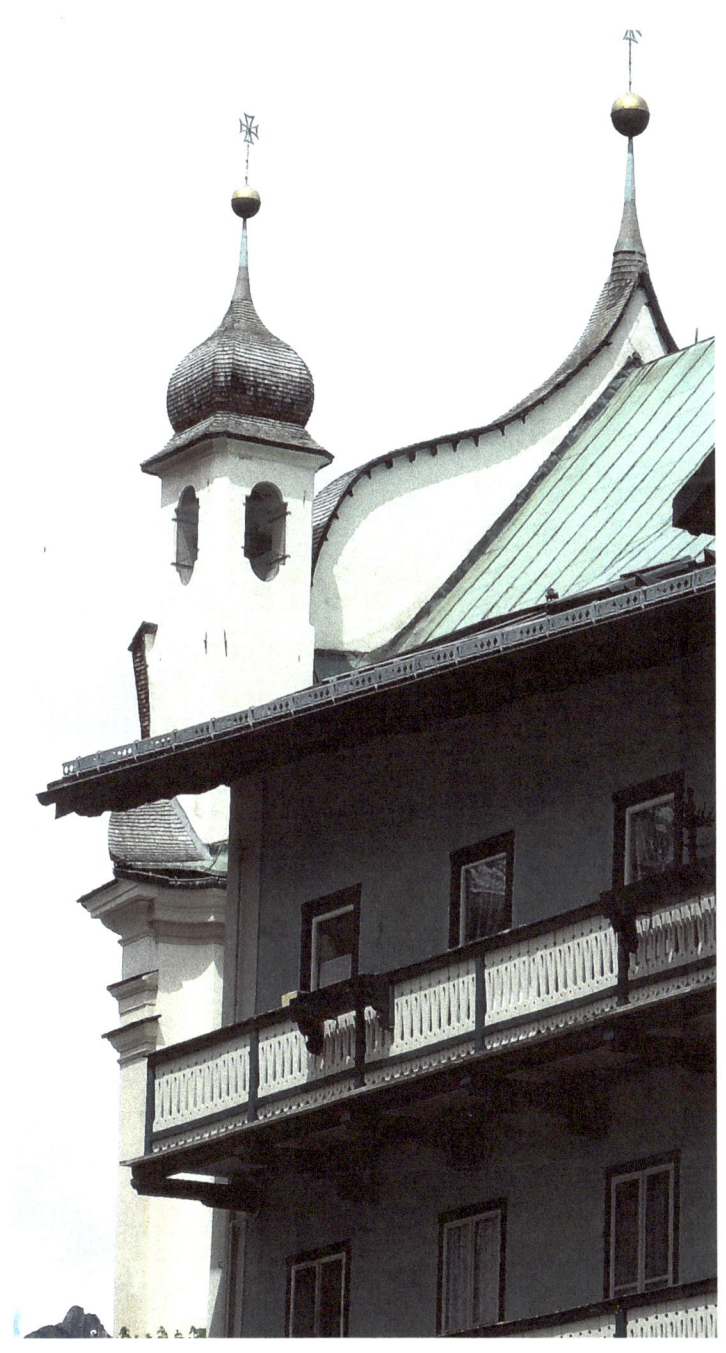

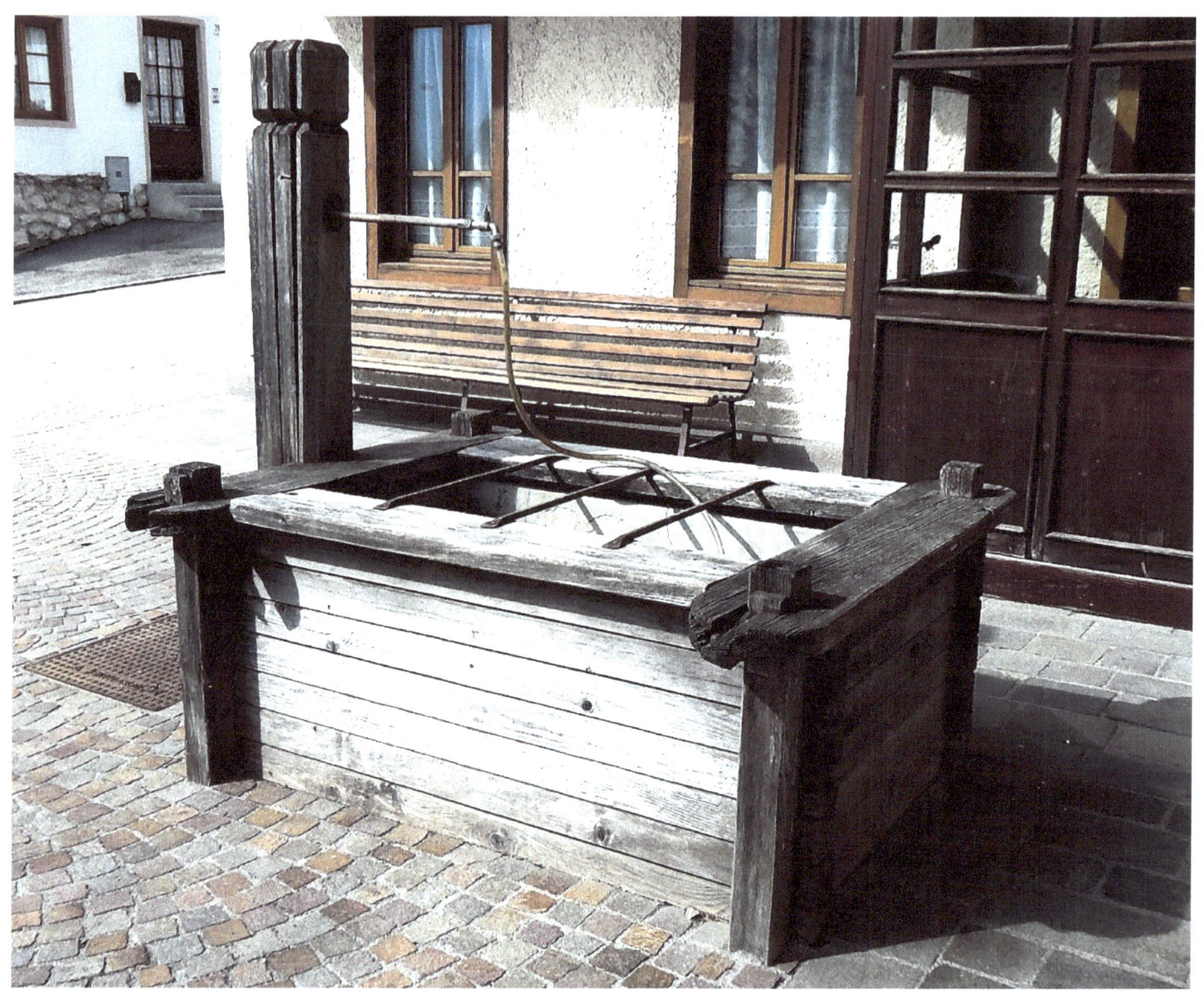

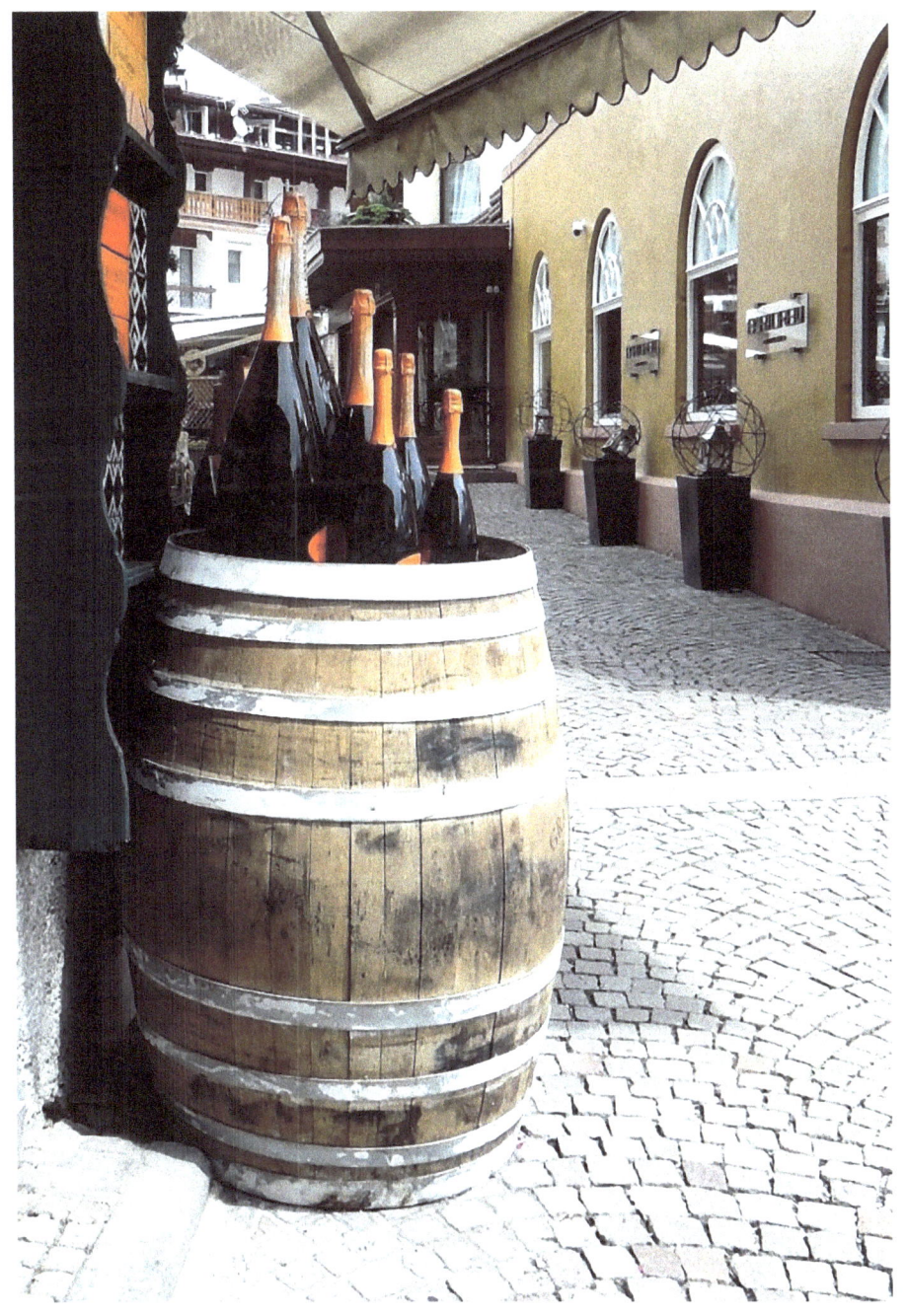

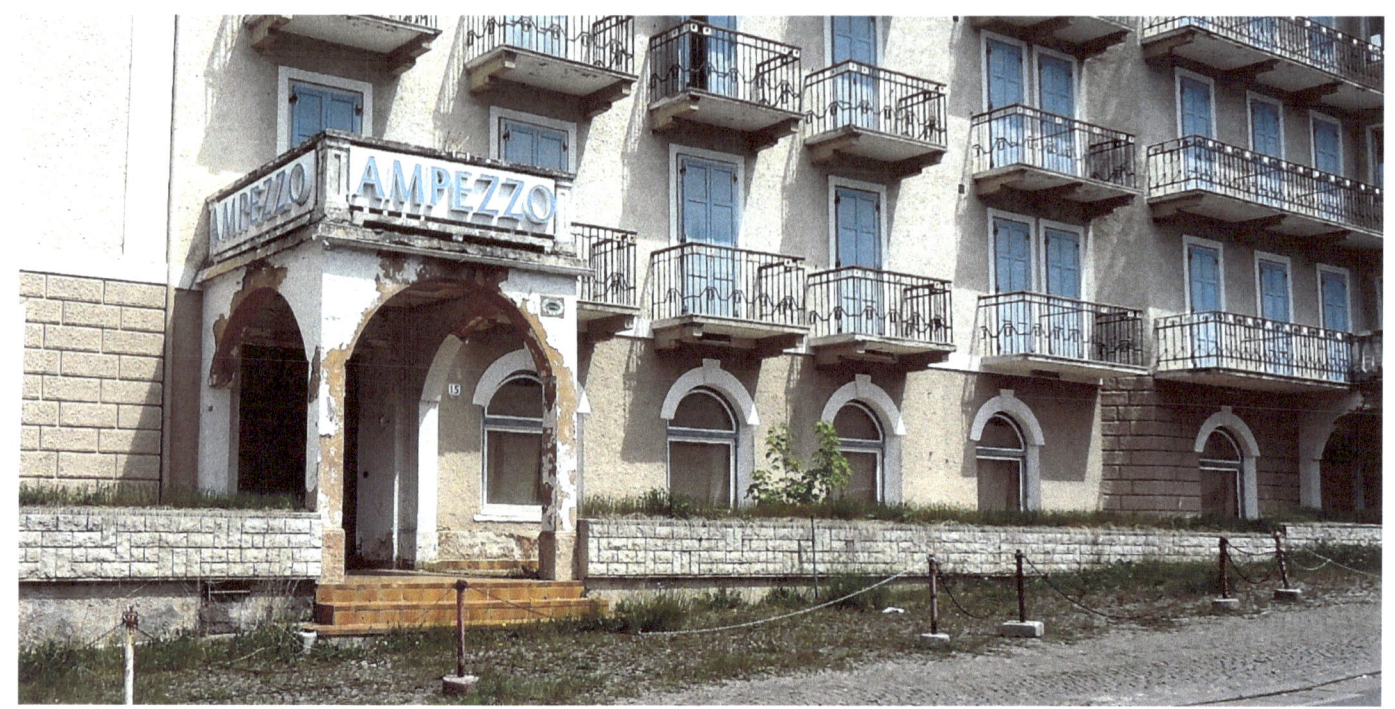

Carfogn, prepare the dough with flour, butter, sugar, whole eggs, egg yolks, white wine and grappa, kneading it well and letting rest at least an hour. Prepare the filling with toasted poppy seeds, sugared and crushed, plus the dark chocolate, biscuits, sugar, milk and brandy. Roll out the dough very thin, fill a canvas pouch with the stuffing and let fall onto the sheet some small nuts to 5-6 cm distance. Cover with another sheet of the same size, cut the carfogns with wheel cutter and fry quickly in hot oil or lard. Finally, sprinkle with powdered sugar.

Fartaies. Beat six eggs well and add one at a time the milk, flour, a small glass of grappa or rum, a tablespoon of icing sugar, half a sachet of baking powder and the grated peel of two lemons, mixing well to obtain a batter soft. Heat plenty of oil in a large, low pan and with the help of a funnel drop the batter into the hot oil starting from the center and moving the funnel in a circular manner, giving the pancake a spiral shape. Fry until golden brown. Dry with baking paper to remove excess oil, sprinkle with icing sugar and serve hot accompanied by cranberry jam.

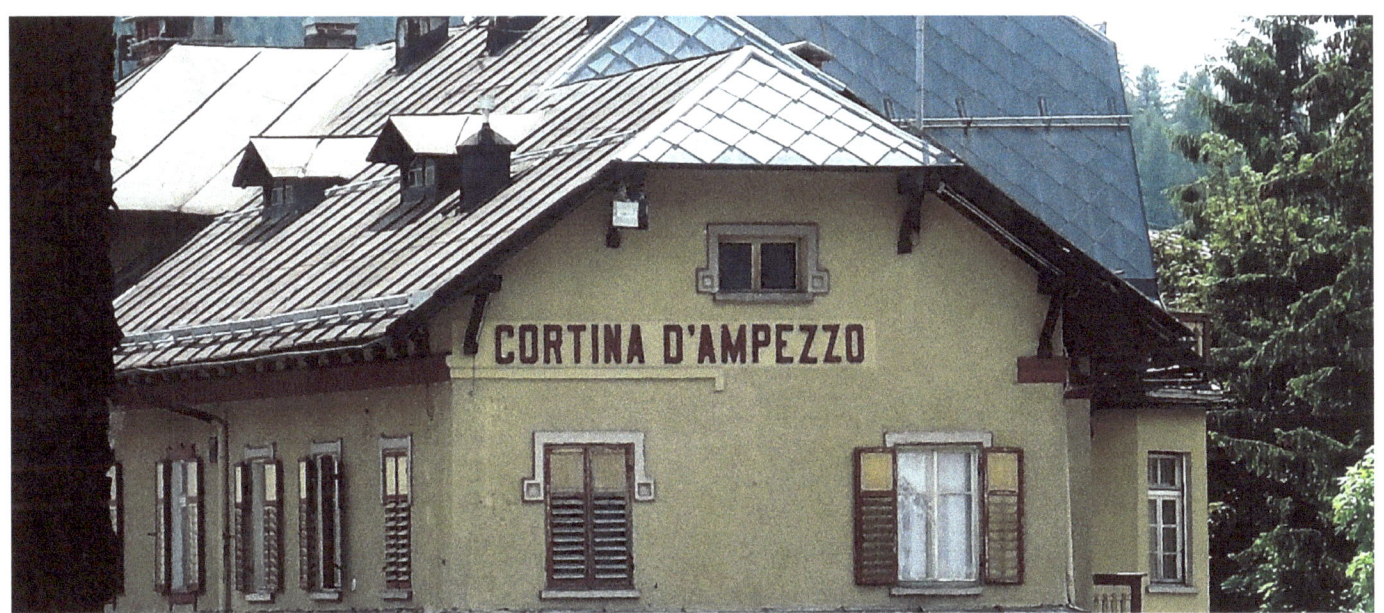

Nighele, fritters of the Ampezzano Carnival. In a bowl incorporate in order one at a time the eggs, sugar, juice and grated peel of an orange and lemon, the rum, a sachet of baking powder, plenty of raisins washed, salt and a glass of milk stirring well with a wooden spoon. Lastly, add the flour a little at a time until you get a consistent dough that remains attached to the spoon. Meanwhile, heat plenty of peanut seed oil in a tall, narrow pan. When the oil is at temperature, make dumplings with the help of two teaspoons soaked in water and dip them directly in the oil. As soon as they have bought a golden color you can drain them and put to dry on a sheet of kitchen paper. Once cooled, sprinkle them with icing sugar.

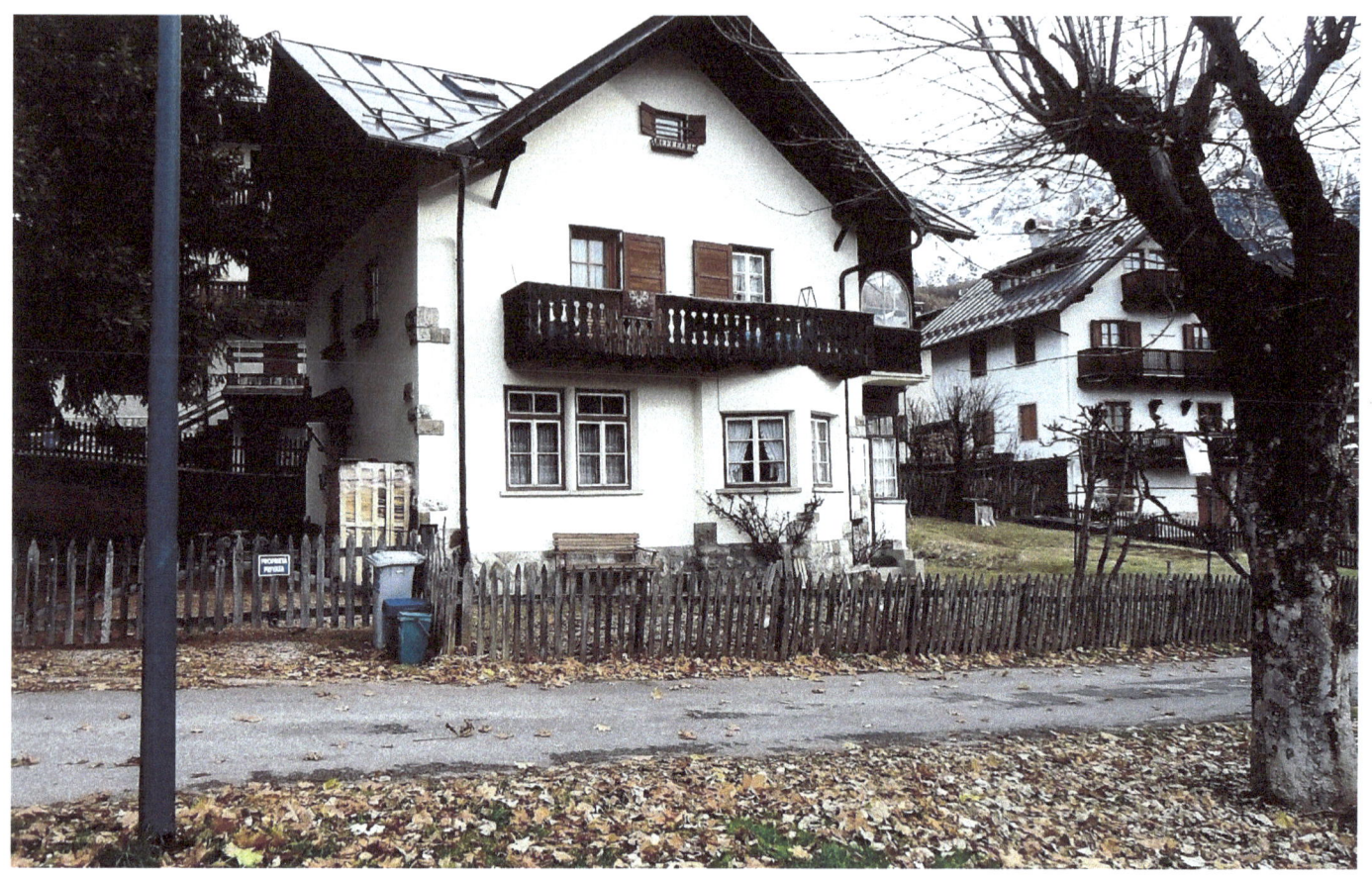

Peta, cadorina cake very soft, made with corn flour and cumin. Whisk the eggs with the sugar and then add the grappa and a pinch of salt. Add the butter into chunks and oil, stirring constantly. Add the corn flour, white flour (double weight of that one of corn) and the yeast to the mixture. Mix well, adding now a bit of cumin. Grease and flour a square baking pan, pour the mixture and bake at 180 degrees for about 45 minutes. Often the basic recipe is enriched as you want with dried figs, raisins or apples.

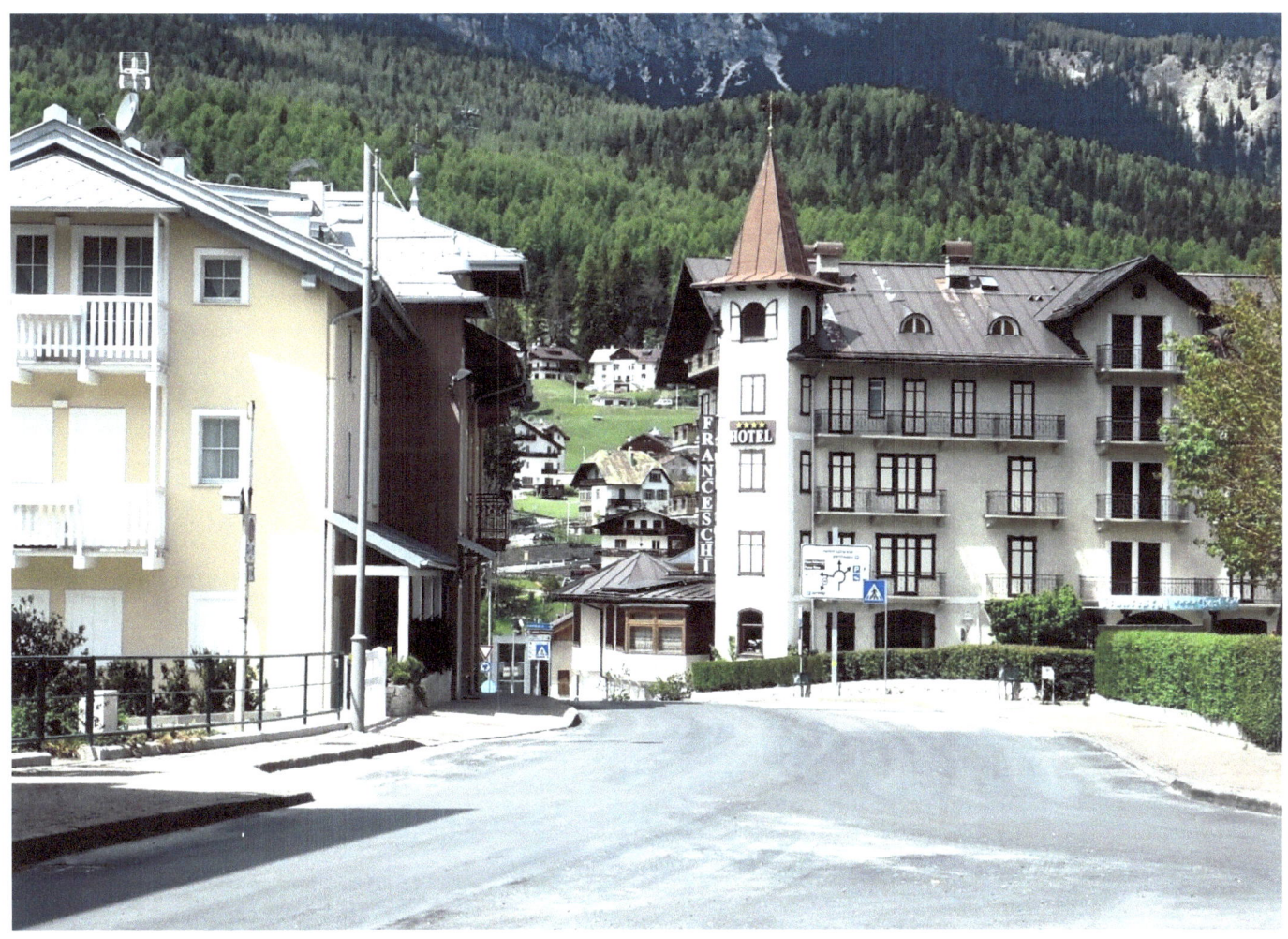

Smòrm con mele, cut the apples into slices and put to macerate with grappa and a little sugar. Separately prepare a thickish batter with flour, eggs, cream, milk, sugar and let stand. In a skillet melt the butter, pour in the batter, put over the apples, brown it well and turn. Finish cooking and break, sprinkle with powdered sugar and serve hot.

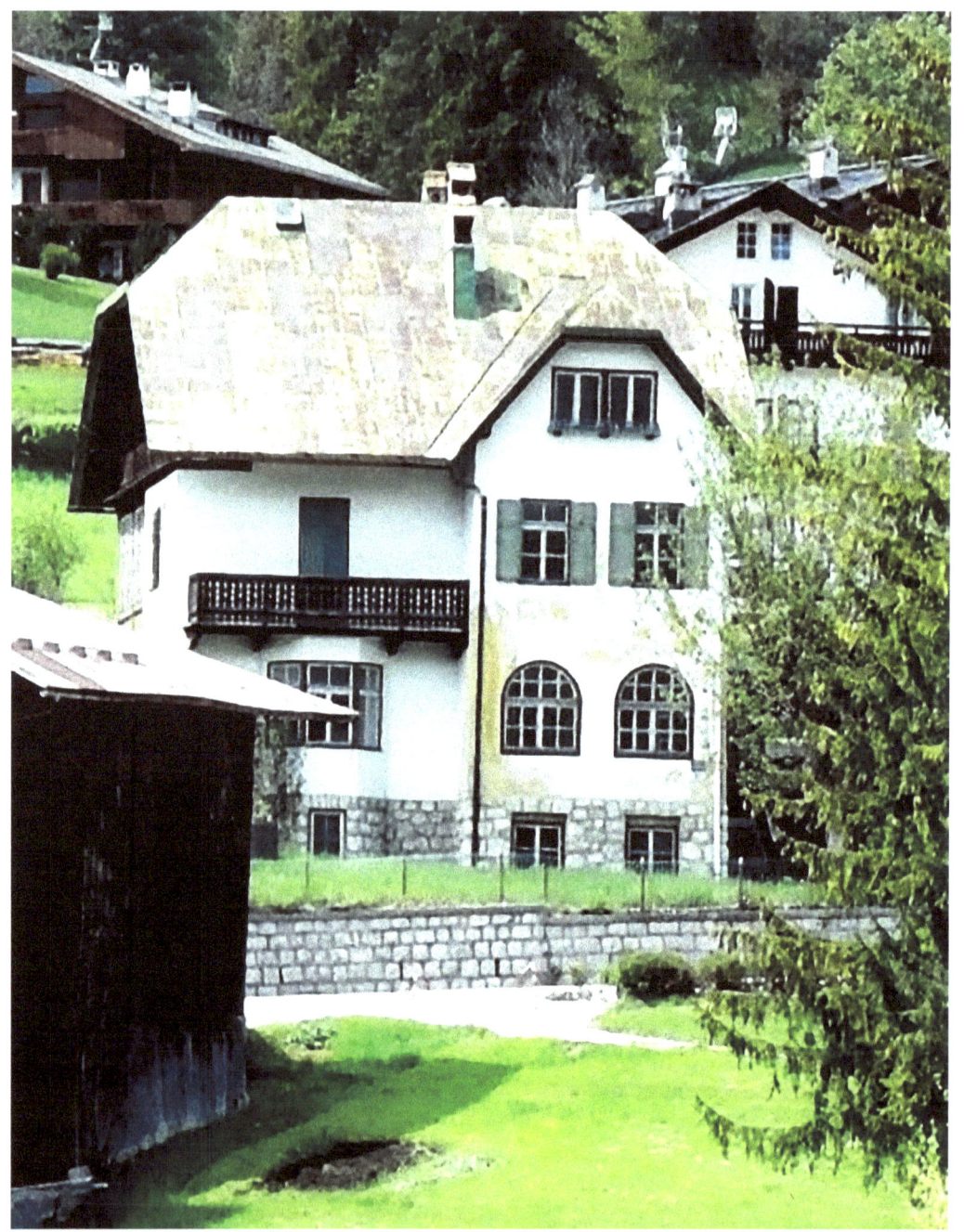

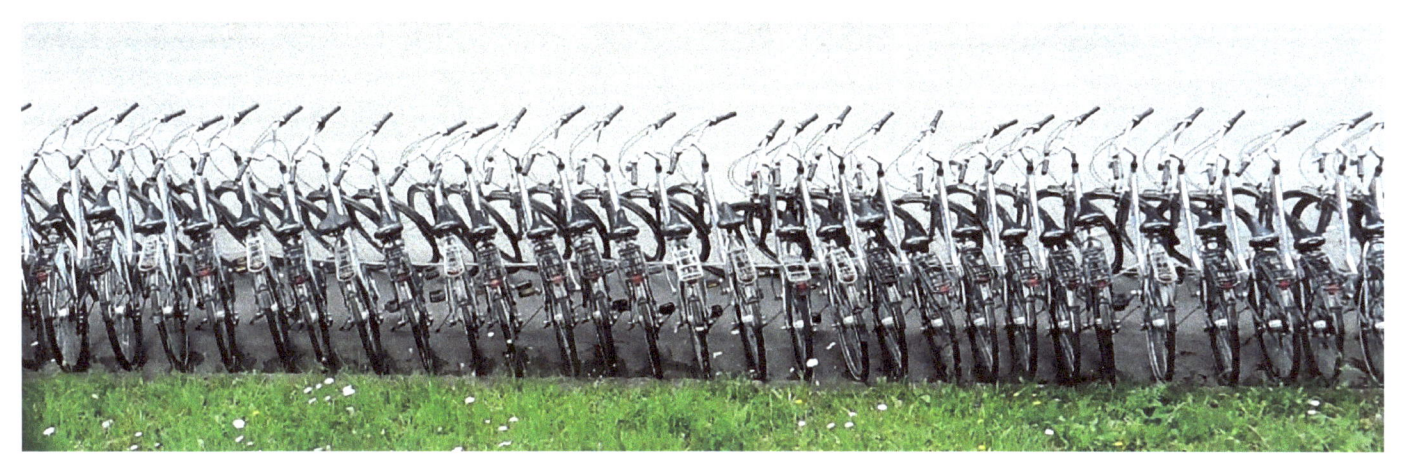

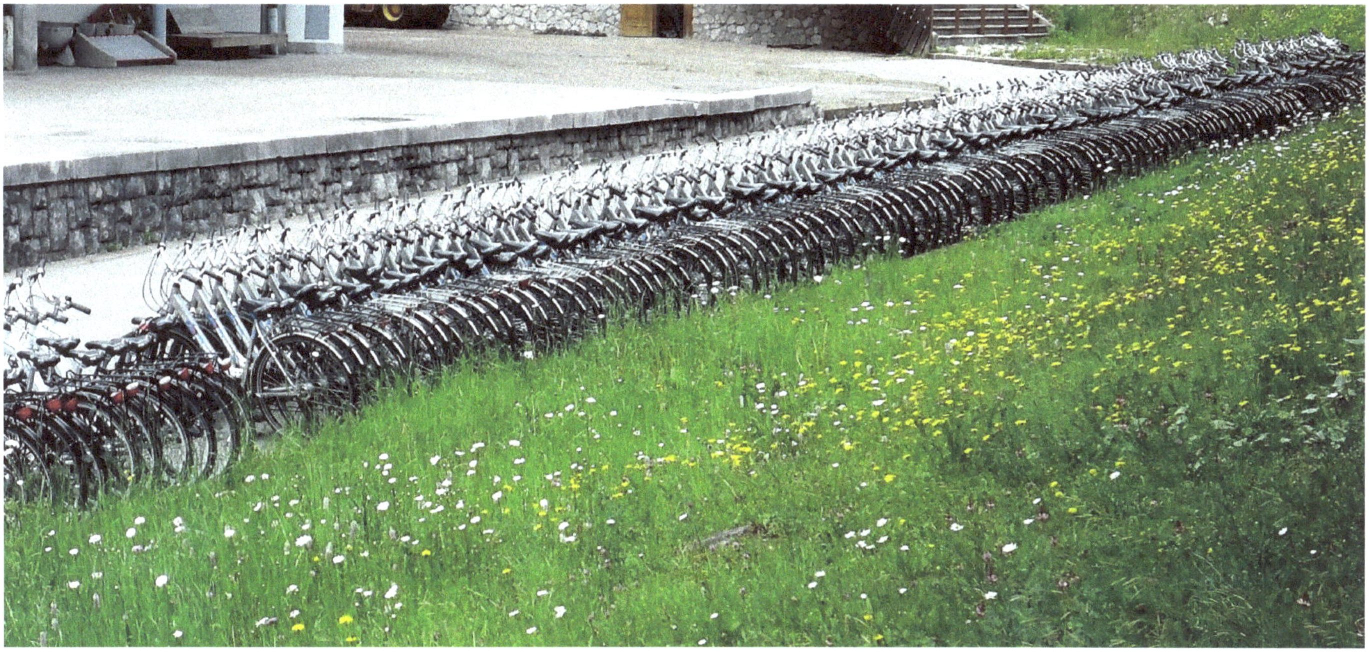

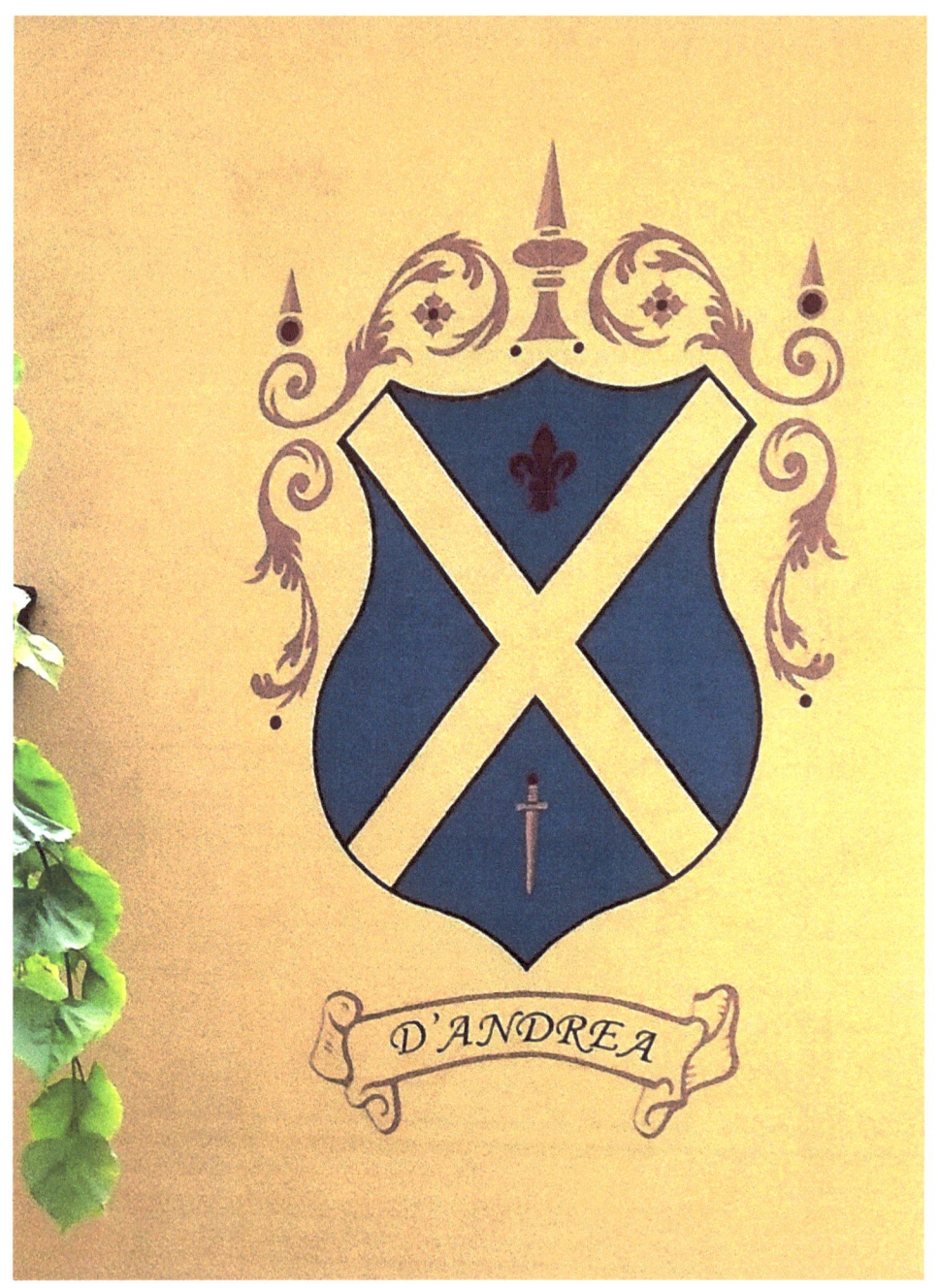

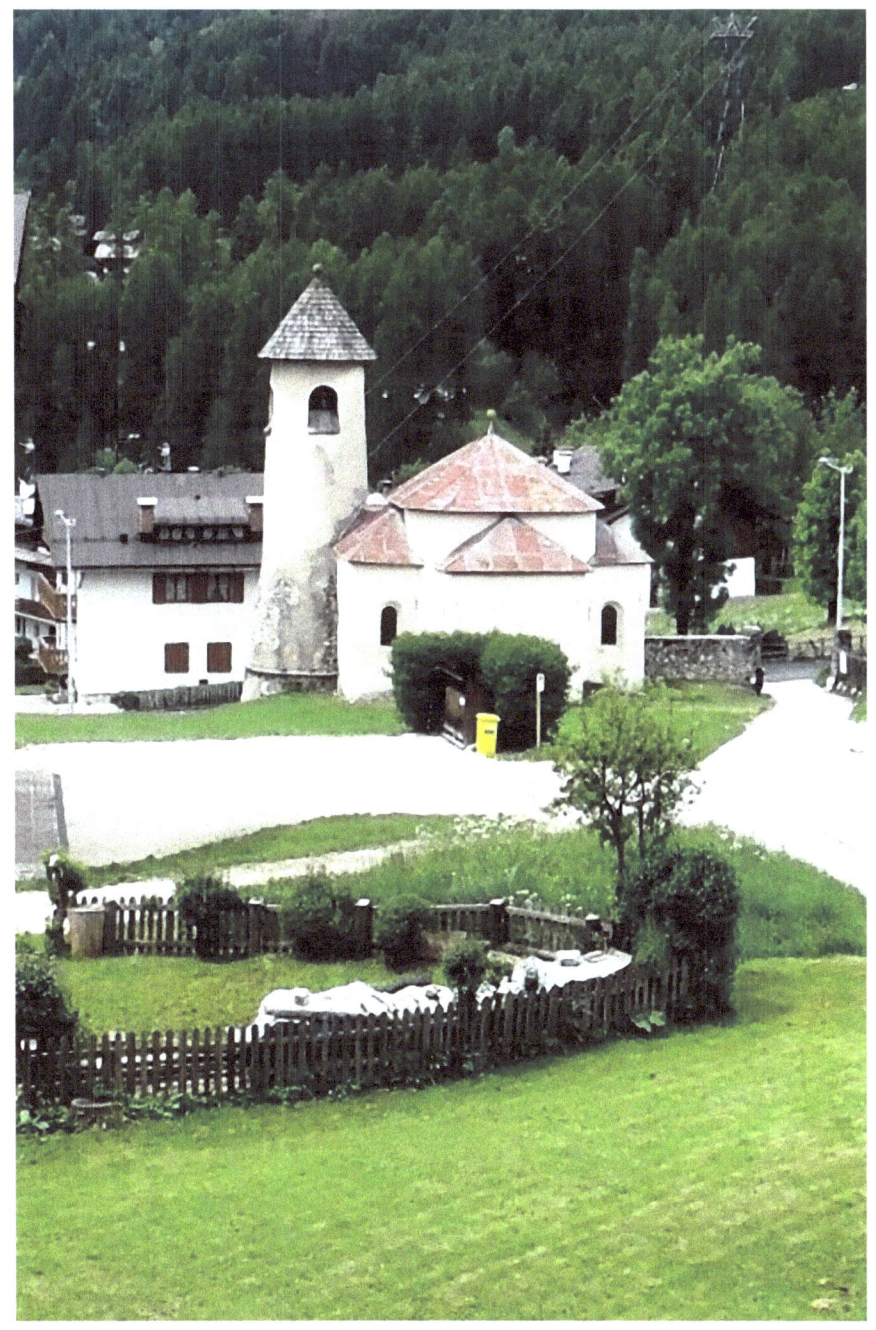

Villa Arianna

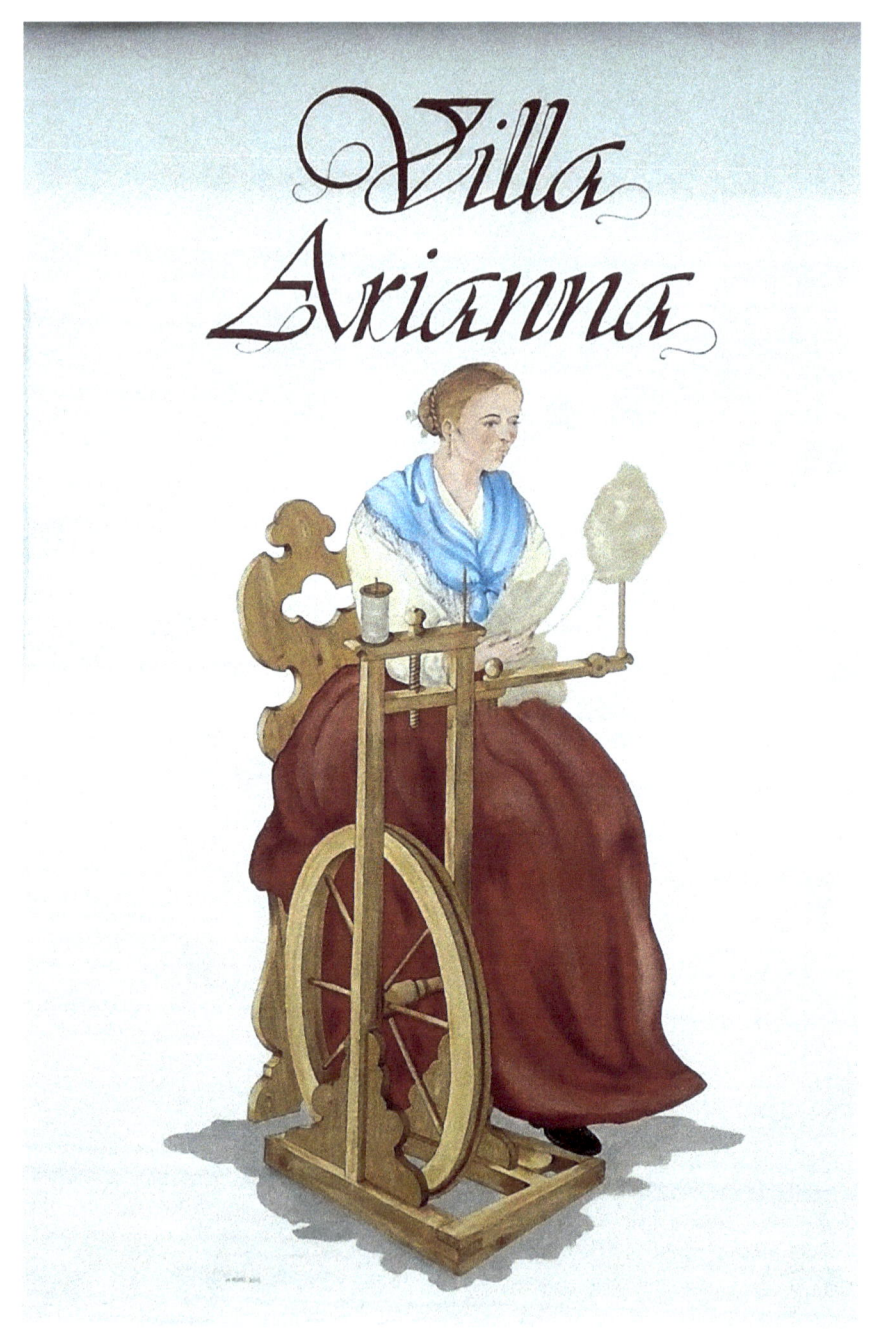

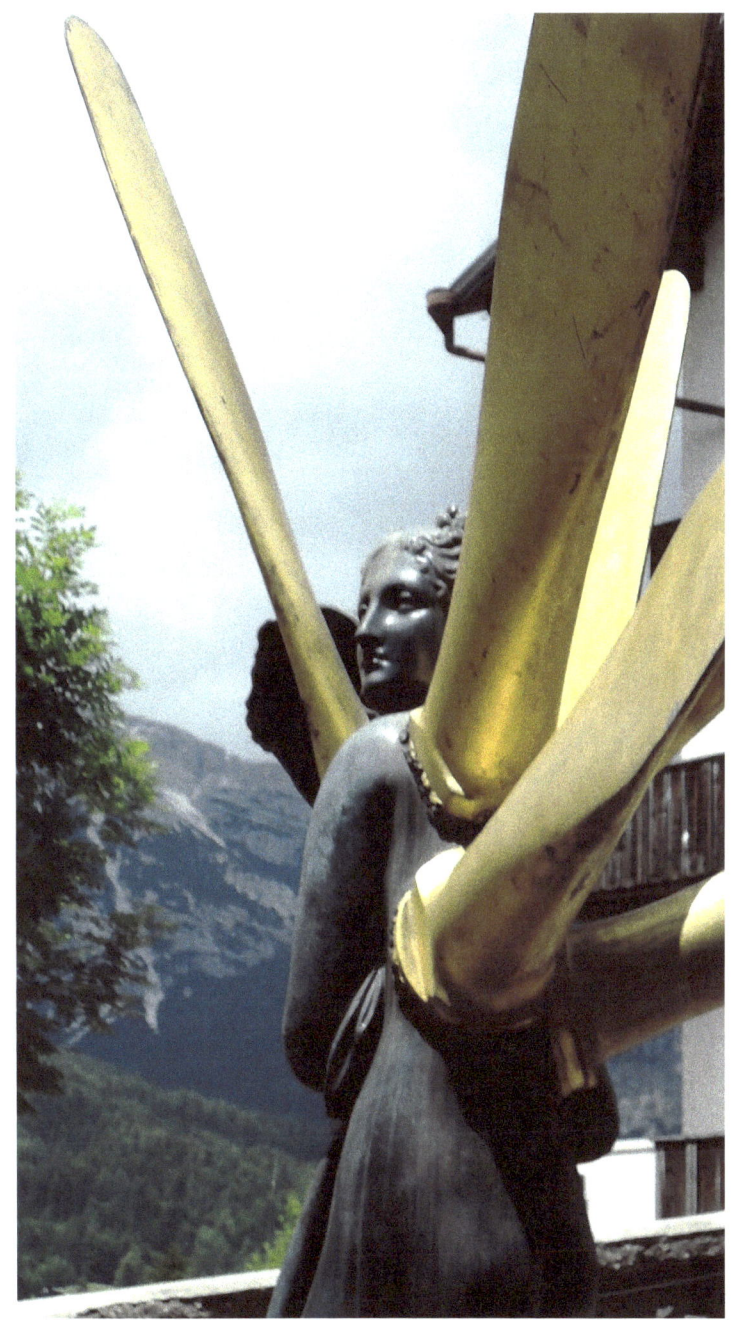

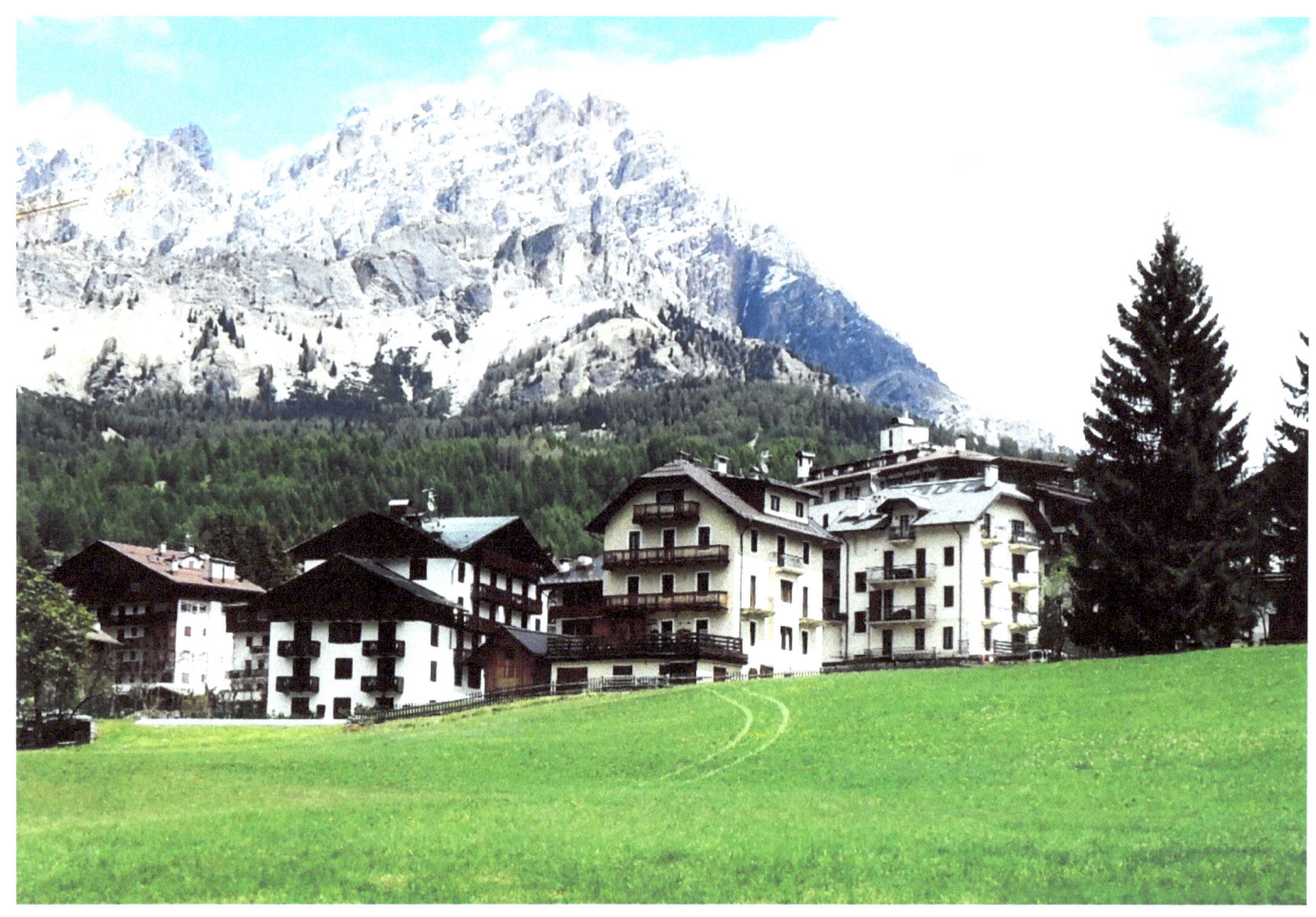

Zopes, cakes made with stale bread, which is soaked in a liquid consisting of wine, eggs, grappa, sugar and browned in butter. Beat the eggs with wine, grappa, sugar and put each slice of bread into this mixture. Melt the butter in a skillet large enough, lay each slice of bread and fry making brown well on both sides. Once cooked, dry the zopes with absorbent kitchen paper and sprinkle with sugar.

Barancio, a very special liquor that is prepared using the resin as a base ingredient and the Mugo pine buds. The tidbits to the Barancio consist of a dish with Barancio, butter, meat and spices. This is a very particular recipe, impossible to find in other areas.

58

www.ingramcontent.com/pod-product-compliance
Lightning Source LLC
Chambersburg PA
CBHW051049180526
45172CB00002B/575